AF646648

BLOOD, CENSORED

BLOOD, CENSORED

When Kashmiris Become the 'Enemy'

DINESH MOHAN, HARSH MANDER, NAVSHARAN SINGH,
PAMELA PHILIPOSE AND TAPAN BOSE

YODAPRESS

79 Gulmohar Enclave
New Delhi 110 049
www.yodapress.co.in

© Dinesh Mohan, Harsh Mander, Navsharan Singh,
Pamela Philipose and Tapan Bose 2018

The moral rights of the author have been asserted
Database right YODA PRESS (maker)

All rights reserved. Enquiries concerning reproduction outside the scope of the above should be sent to YODA PRESS at the address above.

ISBN 978-93-82579-64-9

Editors in charge: Arpita Das and Ishita Gupta
Typeset in Cambria 10/15
By Antara Ghosh
Printed at Replika Press Pvt. Ltd.
Published by Arpita Das for YODA PRESS

Contents

Preface

In July 2016, after security forces killed Hizbul Mujahideen commander, Burhan Wani, the valley of Kashmir went up in flames. We woke up every morning to the troubling news of deaths, blindings, debilitating injuries, arrests and news of angry Kashmiri women and men, many of them young, and of children, pouring out on to the streets across Kashmir. From the tepid public reaction to the public anger and blinding of protestors by pellet guns, in India, it was clear that the Kashmiri people were alone in their suffering. Barring a handful of people's initiatives of solidarity, India remained largely apathetic as Kashmir was wrenched by torment and rage. The people of the Kashmir valley were abandoned not only by their central and state governments in this time of their suffering but also by the Indian civil society which did not seem to care. The mainstream media remained silent or reported on the developments from the prism of 'national security' and not the justice and agony of the Kashmiri people.

A group of friends came together to try to correct this, to break the silences and to demonstrate that we care. Each had past associations with Kashmir–political, emotional, of solidarity, or as human rights workers–and came together, sharing dismay that the people of the Kashmir valley had been abandoned to a repressive security establishment. The high proportion of injuries inflicted on children was of particular concern to all of us. We therefore decided to visit the valley and meet the families and communities that had borne the brunt of state violence as part of a Concerned Citizens' Collective. The five of us who visited Kashmir in December 2016 went on to write this book. We are Tapan Bose, Harsh Mander, Dinesh Mohan, Pamela Philipose and Navsharan Singh.

Tapan Bose, a well-known documentary film-maker, human rights crusader, founder of South Asia Forum for Human Rights and of the Committee for Initiative on Kashmir, has engaged extensively with Kashmir at many different junctures in its violent and troubled history. In March 1990, Tapan Bose, with others, had visited Jammu and Kashmir on a fact-finding mission on behalf of the Committee for Initiative on Kashmir. The mission documented in detail the abuses carried out by the official law-enforcement personnel. They also found that the cases of blatant violation of human rights were not isolated instances or aberrations, but part of official policy. Their report provided a significant first assessment of the ground situation in the valley by an independent group. It appeared in the *Economic and Political Weekly* on 31 March 1991, under the title, 'India's Kashmir War'. Tapan Bose has continued to write and engage with Kashmir.

Harsh Mander, an activist who is well known for his work with survivors of mass violence, has been visiting Kashmir since the mid-2000s, investigating the impact of the two-decade long conflict on children, youth and the everyday lives of ordinary Kashmiris. He has written extensively on the lesser known aspects of Kashmir including the fact that it was one of the most egalitarian societies in the country, in which land reforms were implemented with greater vigour than in most other regions of India. He has also dwelt on the widespread visible poverty in the region and the struggles for livelihood across the valley, pointing to the aching reality of the 'small battles for everyday survival which never cease'.

Dinesh Mohan, Honorary Professor at the Indian Institute of Technology, Delhi, has been active in democratic and human rights movements for several years. He was part of the Committee for Initiative on Kashmir, and a member of the fact-finding team, which produced the report, 'India's Kashmir War' in 1990. He continues to watch Kashmir closely.

Pamela Philipose, journalist, researcher and former director and editor-in-chief of the Women's Feature Service, has been writing on women's experiences of conflict in India as well as the role of the media in responding to crucial contemporary issues. She has highlighted in the media human rights abuses in the Kashmir valley and has been following developments in the region over the years.

Navsharan Singh, an independent researcher and women's rights and human rights practitioner, has been visiting Kashmir since early 2000 as part of the 'Understanding Impunity: Failures and Possibilities of Rights to Truth, Justice and Reparation' initiative. This initiative has documented empirical evidence of systematic and widespread impunity and demonstrated how in widely dissimilar conflict situations, impunity in post-independence India developed along strikingly similar lines. Navsharan Singh's work has focused on understanding impunity specifically with regard to sexual violence, and the meaning of reparations in the context of unrestrained impunity.

As part of the Concerned Citizens' Collective we visited Kashmir from 12 to 16 December 2016, three months after the Burhan Wani assassination, and met a range of people in several parts of the valley from Srinagar to towns and villages in the districts of Kulgam, Pulwama and Anantnag which were most affected. We interacted with over 200 persons; from children disabled by pellets and bullets and their caregivers, to medical doctors from government hospitals, journalists, intellectuals, academics, artistes, lawyers, humanitarian workers, students and members of civil society groups. This was not meant to be a 'fact-finding' visit but a journey of solidarity with the suffering people of Kashmir. It was our way of expressing our pain and outrage at the brutal response of the Indian state to the protests that broke out after the Burhan Wani killing.

On the final day of our visit, we issued a statement detailing what we had seen and heard. What struck us was the complete lack of compassion and the disproportionality of state response to the demonstrations of public anger and outrage across the valley, with stone pelting being met by bullets and pellets. The high proportion of injuries on the faces and upper bodies of the protesters was a clear demonstration that there was official intention to shower hundreds of pellets on the agitated population, not to disperse but to kill or permanently disable.

This attitude of governments, both state and central, we maintained, was even more regrettable because a large majority of the victims of the bullets and pellets were children, many of them so young that they could not have been part of any agitation. Even for those boys who were pelting stones, the response of a democratic state cannot be to disable them for life, or to kill them.

It was also evident to us that there was no display of public compassion by the state government, which had failed to reach out to the children who were blinded and disabled, and their suffering families, many of whom were too frightened to seek medical treatment for fear of being criminalised. At the same time, as a committee we greatly appreciated the doctors and public medical community, including psychiatrists and ophthalmologists, who extended extraordinarily compassionate, even heroic, service and care to the victims of pellet and gun injuries.

We were distressed to learn that many children, arrested as protesters, were incarcerated in adult prisons, while others were detained in juvenile homes but without the protection of a comprehensive juvenile justice system which has not been established in J&K. Equally distressing was our finding that both children and adults were being detained under the draconian anti-democratic Public Security Act.

As a team we found that a wide swathe of public opinion was nearly unanimous in expressing their anguish and alienation from the state. It was clear to us that this was not a movement of militants supported by Pakistan, as was portrayed in the national media, but a broad-based movement comprising almost all sections of Kashmiri society and from all parts of the state.

We could not but express our deep anguish at the suffering of those who we described as our Kashmiri children, sisters and brothers at the hands of a government that is majoritarian, repressive and merciless. We could not but draw parallels with the sense of fear in the valley and that prevailing among minorities, liberals and the poor in other parts of India because of the policies adopted by the central government to its working people and to dissenters.

In our statement at the end of our visit we demanded that pellet guns be banned forthwith and that the leadership of both the central and state governments publicly express regret for the manner in which they were used against children and civilians. We demanded that peaceful dissent and incidents of stone pelting be met with a democratic, proportionate and restrained response from the police and security forces; that security personnel responsible for these excesses and violence face punishment; that the state administration immediately releases all children and youth and political prisoners; that it reaches out with humanity and support to those persons disabled because of bullet and pellet injuries, as well as their caretakers, with necessary provision made available for proper treatment, rehabilitation, education and livelihood opportunities. We were convinced that the way forward was to create a peaceful, just and humane atmosphere in the state by initiating political engagement and meaningful dialogue in order to address the widely held grievances of the people.

This book is the result of that solidarity visit in December 2016, but it encapsulates the experiences and understanding of years of engagement with Kashmir by the members of the collective. We wrote this book because we felt it was important to document this particular period in the long, troubled history of Kashmir because it marked for us a distinct phase of repression; a phase that saw targeted killings as well as injuries and blindings in flagrant defiance of humanitarian concerns and international norms on the treatment of civilian populations in conflict zones. The state's belligerent refusal to initiate dialogue unless the Kashmiri people capitulated unconditionally was a blot on Indian democracy.

We write this with a hope that the larger civil society in India will take time to ponder over how the ruling dispensation has successfully, and cynically, converted the real concerns of the people of Kashmir into 'problems', and how these 'problems' were turned into festering wounds. The multiple tragedies that emerged as a result are poignantly reflected in the faces of young children blinded and scarred for life.

Tapan Bose, Harsh Mander, Dinesh Mohan,
Pamela Philipose, Navsharan Singh

December 2017

I

Sightless Autumn: Kashmir 2016

I will die, in autumn, in Kashmir,
and the shadowed routine of each vein will almost be news,
the blood censored...

– Agha Shahid Ali

What do the ordinary people do when they become 'enemy people' in the eyes of the state, when the line between countryman and enemy, civilian and insurgent, blurs away, when violence is routinised and made normal and, citizens, including children, are brutally targeted by a legally unencumbered state? When the hostility against certain people is not limited to the state, but also extends to society, citizens and public institutions, what do the ordinary people do? In situations, when there is evidence of individuals being disappeared, tortured, killed in custody and raped, and explained away either as 'aberrations' or condoned in the interest of a 'greater cause', what do the Kashmiri people do?

This is a troubling question outside the familiar zone of rule of law-determined solutions. Talking about rule of law and freedoms is reassuring when we know we can bring to the discussions ways in which we can protect what needs protection, i.e., all citizens' rights and dignity. Accepting that we live in a country where the rights of certain people are routinely violated is hard for many to admit, but perhaps what is harder to swallow is that not only are rights pulverised, it is the custodian of the law of the land which stands accused for these violations. When we hear about lines being crossed and rights violated at a large scale, we are anguished but also filled with the expectation that the wrong will be righted. But when it doesn't happen, and impunity systematically erodes the constitutional provisions and values, denial of redress works as a double betrayal of the sense of justice: a violation has occurred and what is more, it has not been rectified, worse still, it is justified. In this situation what do the Kashmiri people do? This is a question staring us in our faces.

The valley of Kashmir has long been in turmoil, but it probably never smouldered with such combustible public rage as it does today. In the 1990s, the uprising in the Kashmir valley was fuelled by militants supported, trained and armed by the Pakistani establishment. But after an entire generation of Kashmiris have grown up only under the shadow of the gun, the revolt has transformed increasingly into a mass movement. The government itself admits that the number of militants in Kashmir are only a few hundred. But young people in Kashmir have lost their fear of the soldier and the gun. They are spilling in thousands onto the streets, and there is no part of the valley that is untouched by their rage.

In the winter of 2016, the writers of this book visited the Kashmir valley—lacerated, wrathful, aflame—for solidarity and fact-finding. It was a journey of shame and outrage, and a sadness that does not let us be. This is why we write this book.

We encountered numerous young people blinded by pellets, and others with bullet injuries in their skulls and legs. Some of those felled and blinded may have been among the thousands who pelted stones on the soldiers and policepersons who tried to block their processions. They too should not have been laid down by their country's soldiers. But many were too young to have even understood what was happening. Their families were utterly devastated with the suffering of many who were still children. The wanton blinding by security forces of children has wounded the souls of the Kashmiri people in ways that little else has in their long turbulent past. The question that people asked us over and over again was this: 'You say we are equal citizens of India. Yes, some of our boys pelted stones. But we know of far more violent mobs in other parts of India this last year—the Jat and Patidar agitations, the Cauvery dispute and many others. To disperse those mobs, have security forces ever used pellet guns? In all those unrests, lathis, tear-gas and water-cannons were found to be sufficient by India's security establishment. But why is it that only for Kashmiri youth throwing stones, you use pellet guns?'

The gun has long been deployed by the Indian state to try to cow down and silence the defiant and rebellious Kashmiri. But with it there has also been dialogue and the political process. The policy of the Indian government led by Narendra Modi towards the people of Kashmir has hardened into one of unmitigated militarism—subjugation, submission and only then dialogue. The government had made it clear that it is prepared to continue to blind, disable or even kill its youth if they try to fight the army with stones, or they have the misfortune of being part of an angry crowd, or just an onlooker. The army chief General Bipin Rawat repeatedly threatens 'tough action' against even those who abjure the gun, declaring that those who pelt stones will be treated as overground supporters of militants and they will have to face the full brunt of the formidable military power of the Indian state. The signs are unmistakable that the government is almost in a state of undeclared war against its own people.

India's army chief declared that the government is prepared to give those who support terror activities an opportunity to join the 'national mainstream', but warned that if they continued their actions, security forces would respond with 'harsher measures'. 'They may survive today but we will get them tomorrow. Our relentless operations will continue.' He added that the army would go 'helter-skelter' against local boys who pick up arms or aid besieged militants.

* * *

The nature of political contestation in the Kashmir valley has transformed greatly from the 1990s. The militant insurgency of the 1990s buttressed from across the border, has increasingly given way to indigenous mass civilian protests after 2008. To disperse such throngs of civilian protesters the government has relied on mostly lethal and repressive strategies, resulting in large numbers of mostly civilian deaths. The years 2008 and 2010 were especially volatile and saw months-long mass protests at a stretch, resulting in almost 60 deaths in 2008 and 120 deaths in 2010. Between 2010 and 2016, the ongoing intense conflict was concentrated in only some of the pockets in Kashmir especially in four districts of South Kashmir. However, the entire valley of Kashmir has witnessed mass protests and the longest curfew that the valley has ever seen, for almost five months at a stretch from 8 July 2016 onwards.

The killing of 22-year-old militant Burhan Wani by security forces became a rallying point for public anguish and rage across the Kashmir valley on a scale that few could have predicted. Infuriated crowds joined massive funeral processions and protest marches across the valley, as security forces fired at them with volleys of rifles and pellet guns, blinding and killing protestors and bystanders, many of them very young. Instead of quelling the revolt, the military response of the state led only to further inflaming public wrath, and a cycle of defiant protests, mass processions, more killings, blindings and arrests, persisted for several months.

More than 90 people died and over 15,000 people were injured.[1] Around 1100 people suffered pellet injuries in their eyes, resulting in the loss of one or both eyes of at least 500 people; a situation which the *New York Times* narrated as an 'epidemic of dead eyes in Kashmir'.[2] A significant proportion of those injured by pellets were below 15 years of age.[3] Children as young as 4 years old were hit by pellets. In addition, thousands of people were arrested, including children, both by legal process and outside it. The militarisation of a region which anyway is one of the most militarised in the world has further

---

1 *Greater Kashmir*, 20 November 2016 https://www.theguardian.com/world/2016/nov/08/india-crackdown-in-kashmir-is-this-worlds-first-mass-blinding

2 *New York Times*, 29 August 2016.

3 *The Hindu*, 22 August 2016.

mounted with more than an additional 100 companies of para-military forces being moved to Kashmir.[4]

A fact-finding team of 25 citizens, including activists Medha Patkar, Kavita Krishnan, Anuradha Bhasin, the editor of *Kashmir Times*, human rights groups from Nagaland, and others from trade unions and people's movements across the country, visited the valley for nine days in November 2016. We rely here on a detailed report on the findings of this group published in *Scroll*.[5] It charged that the deaths and blindings in these months were the result of deliberately targeted killings and injuries by security forces, as most deaths were 'caused by injuries waist-above, without any warning fire'. The report records many human rights abuses. The Jammu and Kashmir police lodged 'cross' FIRs or counter-complaints. Most of these bore the same charge: the victim was 'anti-national'. It records that families who tried to take legal recourse against security forces were harassed, tortured and arrested. It describes the death of a boy in Kupwara district who was allegedly killed by a known police officer but the FIR was filed against 'unknown security persons'. It also describes the incident of a boy who was allegedly shot with pellets and drowned in a nullah in Qazigund in Anantnag district. The counter-FIR filed by the police in this case speaks of a large, violent mob, armed with stones and petrol bombs, attacking members of the Central Reserve Police Force, 'with the intention to cause death'. The boy, according to this FIR, was 'critically injured' when forces tried to disperse the crowd using tear gas and loudspeakers. His family insists that he was not part of the protests.[6]

Since Wani's killing, the fact-finding citizens' team claims that about 16,000 people were arrested or detained. These include 600 people who were booked under the Public Safety Act, a law which enables police officials to detain individuals on grounds that can be withheld. Those held are judged by the police to be a threat to 'public order' or to the 'security of the state'.

---

4 *Greater Kashmir*, 26 September 2016.

5 Security forces conducted targeted killings during 2016 protests, alleges citizens report – https://scroll.in/article/837310/kashmir-security-forces-conducted-targeted-killings-during-2016-protests-alleges-citizens-report

6 Ibid.

A person so detained may be held for up to two years. According to the report, those detained under the law in 2016 included 'minors, government and security personnel, human rights activists, lawyers and the physically disabled'. These included even, in the old town of Baramulla, a 27-year-old mechanic who cannot walk without crutches and also suffers from visual and hearing impairments.[7] They found that a stone mason who had been wounded with pellets was not allowed treatment for his wounds. This man from Khanpora in Baramulla district, the team said, was booked under the act. He had been detained under the Public Safety Act three times before, in 2008, 2010 and 2012. It was because of his record that he was denied treatment. Members of the Jammu and Kashmir Bar Association spoke to the team of 'several delay tactics employed by government authorities to prolong periods of detention, including charging civilians under multiple "open" FIRs, in which people can be implicated in cases even after years of filing the FIR, and delays in filing responses on PSA cases in courts.'

The 2016 unrest has probably seen the longest ever span of curfews imposed and strikes at a stretch in Kashmir's history, and also the worst in terms of the casualties and devastation it has resulted in. Its intensity can be understood by the fact that more than 800 stone pelting incidents were reported during the month of July and more than 700 in the month of August and almost every road inside rural and urban areas was closed. Mobile and internet services were banned, resulting in almost a communication blackout. In the first two months of unrest between 8 July and 8 September, 166 people were injured every day, on an average.[8] All this created a very fearful and insecure environment, and as a result, social and economic life came to a complete halt in Kashmir during these five months.

The shut-down and curfews led to the closure of schools, businesses, markets and almost all employment opportunities. Many government services related to nutrition and employment including ICDS (Integrated Child Development Services), MDMS (Mid Day Meal Scheme), MGNREGA

7 Ibid.

8 Greater Kashmir, 8 September 2016.

(Mahatma Gandhi National Rural Employment Guarantee Act) and other public works also completely collapsed. This took a particularly heavy toll on the poor, including farmers and daily wagers and also groups like the aged and disabled. This led to a crisis in the access to adequate food of many such households. Action Aid conducted a survey in South Kashmir's two districts of Anantnag and Kulgam covering a total of 167 households, spread across urban as well as rural areas, with a focus on the vulnerable and poor population in the first week of September 2016. Ninety-eight per cent of the households reported in the survey that the quantity of their meals had reduced after the unrest started in the valley. To meet the food needs, 43 per cent of households had reported that they borrowed ration (on debt) from local shopkeepers. Further, almost 81 per cent reported they didn't get any work post unrest (for almost two months at a stretch by the time of this survey) because of insecurity, curfews and lack of transport facilities, which restricted the mobility of people. To cope and manage their living, 66 per cent had borrowed money and 6 per cent said they had to sell items/ assets.This deterioration in people's accessibility to food and livelihoods became even more damaging especially because the people of the state were yet to fully recover from the economic effects of the 2014 floods, which had damaged more than two lakh structures and had also affected access of thousands of households to food, livelihood, safe drinking water, health and hygiene, and sanitation.

Many hoped that this period of prolonged violence and suffering would be followed by an interregnum of peace. People, even angry and alienated people, have to live, to earn, to study, and to feed their children. But as soon as the snows melted in early 2017, the Indian state made it clear that it would continue its policy of maximum force against the uprising of Kashmiri people, and bullets, pellets and stones began to fly again.

Tommy Wilkes and Fayaz Bukhari of *Reuters* reported in the summer of 2017 that 'Images of students confronting police on campuses have come to symbolise Kashmiri protests against Indian rule as much as gun-toting militants in fatigues, in what security officials and separatist leaders say is a dangerous new phase of the conflict. The sharp rise in violence in recent weeks is more spontaneous than before, complicating the task of Indian security forces trained largely in counter-insurgency and poorly equipped to contain broader unrest.' They reported that security forces entered a college in March 2017 in Pulwama to arrest suspected agitators. Hundreds of students responded by throwing stones at their vehicles 'before fighting pitched battles inside college corridors and bathrooms. Within days, widespread protests forced most colleges and secondary schools in Indian-controlled Kashmir to close. Teenaged girls took to the streets for the first time in years. At least 100 protesters were wounded.'

The ordinary people of the Kashmir valley have been abandoned by their central and state governments. The only face of government that the people encounter is of the security establishment. There is no proportionality of state response as stone pelting is met by bullets and pellet guns. The high proportion of injuries on the face and above the waist demonstrate that there was official intention to shower hundreds of pellets, not to disperse but to kill or permanently disable the agitated populations. It is clear that the government and its security establishment is using forms and levels of state violence in the Kashmir valley that it has not deployed in other parts of the country that have also seen even more violent agitations in recent months, and even less in the growing rash of incidents of mob lynching in which the police merely stands by. This highly excessive use of force against the Kashmiri people reflects an attempt to crush their spirit and treat them almost like an enemy population.

This attitude of governments is even more regrettable because the large majority of victims of the bullets and pellet guns are children, many of them so young that they could not have been part of any agitation. Even for those underage boys who were pelting stones, the response of a democratic state cannot be to disable them for life, or to kill them. There is also no display of public compassion by the state government, which has not reached out to the children who are blinded and disabled, and their suffering families are sometimes scared to seek medical treatment for fear of being criminalised. We also deplore the finding that many children are being picked up from classrooms in schools and colleges, held illegally for days in police stations and army camps, incarcerated in adult prisons or in juvenile homes even though there is no effective architecture of a juvenile justice system in J&K.

The ever-hardening militarist policy of the Indian state to the Kashmiri people grows out of their conviction that public anger is being fuelled and organised by Pakistan. This gives Pakistan far more credit (or discredit) than is due to it! When senior politicians and officials seriously make the charge that stone-pelters are paid 500 rupees a day to throw stones at armed soldiers, they are either deliberately closing their eyes to the surge, scale and spread of public anger in the valley, or they are simply satisfying their hyper-nationalist constituency.

WHAT MAKES THE PRESENT PHASE OF VIOLENCE DIFFERENT?

During the debate in Parliament on 20 July 2016 regarding the situation in Kashmir, when opposition parties condemned the use of excessive force by the security forces, several members of the BJP supported the security forces on the ground, stating that they were fighting against Pakistan-sponsored 'terrorism'. The Home Minister claimed, 'Our neighbour is conspiring to disturb the situation in the Kashmir valley in the name of the religion.' The Home Minister refuted the charges of use of excessive force on protesting civilians. The Finance Minister Mr Arun Jaitley claimed that in Jammu and Kashmir it was a battle between the country and Pakistan-sponsored separatist forces.

Whenever charged by opposition parties and critics for using excessive force against civilian populations, the defence mounted by the government and its many supporters, including those in television studios, is always that they are unwilling to be weak in their response to terrorism. But what we see dominating and sweeping Kashmir today is not terrorism or militancy. It is a mass rebellion. Army sources themselves estimate that there are no more than 500 militants in Kashmir today, as against ten to twenty times that number at the peak of militancy in the 1990s. The ever-growing flood of children, young people, women and men that we see pouring into the streets of every corner of Kashmir today have not picked up arms. The most lethal weapon that they hold is stones, and their rage.

Pakistan did play a central role in Kashmiri militancy in its high noon of the 1990s. As senior journalist Prem Shankar Jha observes, 'Pakistan trained hundreds of young Kashmiris in the mujahid training camps it had set up for Afghans and funnelled more than 5,000 small arms into the Valley. But today, it is a default assumption that starkly highlights the bankruptcy of understanding in the BJP.'[9]

Those who visited the valley in the early 1990s, when the movement for 'self-determination' began, may still see some glimpses of the past in today's protests. However, there are two major differences. Unlike the earlier movement, which was dominated by armed groups, the current movement for *azadi* does not deploy guns, except for a small band of indigenous insurgents. There may have been support among sections of the Kashmiri population for the men who picked up arms in the 1990s, but they did not spill onto the streets, as they do today, in their thousands. And second, the 'jihadi' the 'mujahedeen' or 'militants'—classified as 'terrorists' by the Indian government—are almost nowhere in the picture. The current protests have been launched by the local youth and led by locals, rendering the so-called 'separatists' almost irrelevant.

The difference between the 1990s and now, as Prem Shankar Jha observes, is that 'three-quarters of today's Kashmiris have known only the coercive face of Indian democracy—distrust and animosity have therefore struck deep roots within them.'[10]

Shoaib Daniyal agrees, 'The current conflict is different. While the 1990s saw militants take on Indian armed forces, 2017 has seen an unprecedented mass mobilisation. This has involved large crowds hurling stones at the security forces—an activity so widespread that even teenage girls have participated in it. When the security forces battle militants, crowds in Kashmir frequently head towards encounter sites and attempt to disrupt them.... Kashmir's anger is so intense, the state's political presence has nearly faded out.'[11]

---

9 Prem Shankar Jha, 'For Kashmir's Future', *Indian Express*, 27 May 2017.

10 Ibid.

11 https://scroll.in/article/836299/the-daily-fix-modi-governments-muscular-policy-is-leading-to-disaster-in-kashmir

This is a generation that has only seen a Kashmir with the soldier never far from their line of sight and daily lived experience. This is the Kashmir of their fathers and brothers—subjected to public beatings, humiliation, during the much-dreaded 'crackdowns' on Kashmiri urban neighbourhoods and villages.[12] It is the Kashmir of soldiers entering homes and destroying everything. It is the Kashmir of summary executions, of enforced disappearances, of rape, of check-posts at every turn with no young Kashmiri without a personal story of humiliation, and loss.

Even in small towns, you encounter bulletproof tanks stationed on busy market squares, and surly soldiers armed with deadly weapons at every turn. The soldiers themselves dread their postings to Kashmir. Separated from their families, they said: 'We are lonely. We detest the winter cold, and the long hours. We are forced to stand at our posts with our guns from early morning to late into the night. But worse still is that the local people hate us so much. We are therefore always worried for our lives.'[13]

One of the authors of this book recounts excerpts from his record of meeting several hundred young people in Kashmir.[14] 'My earliest memory is to wake up one night suddenly to find strange men in uniforms with guns had broken into my parents' bedroom, where I also sleep,' recalled a university student from Srinagar. 'I was only seven then', she adds, 'but my childhood ended from that day. My mother tried to run towards me to protect me, but the soldier stopped her harshly warning, "Don't move, or you will be shot. You will die like a bitch." These were his exact words. I tried to still go to my mother, but the soldier grabbed me by my hair. Thirteen years later, I can still feel the pain of his rough grasp of my hair. It burns my soul. My father was enraged to see the soldier pull my hair and tried to run towards him. The soldier raised his rifle to his chest and pulled the trigger. The gun jumped, and my father was barely saved. I feel terrified when I remember that day's events to this day.' They were all dragged out of the house, charged with giving food and shelter to militants. For a year, the nightmare continued,

---

12 'Indian Masculinity, Nationalism, and Torture Videos from Kashmir' in Raiot – http://raiot.in/indian-masculinity-nationalism-and-torture-videos-from-kashmir/

13 HM in *the Hindu*

14 HM in *the Hindu*

with one or the other adult at home being arrested, and constant raids and searches in their home.

Many youths talked of mass graves and custodial killings; of fathers who were 'disappeared' by security forces, picked up, and the family's aching wait for them who would never return. A young shawlmaker, Shafi, spoke of three brothers in his village whose father 'disappeared', and all the boys became thieves. 'Without fathers to guide them, so many boys have become *awaralafanga* (vagabonds),' adds another. One college student said that his father was in custody for long stretches, because he was suspected of sympathising with militant groups. 'As a child, I was often angry with my father, because I felt he had brought us so much suffering. I would not even talk to him. But now in college, I endorse his beliefs.' They all spoke also of despair breeding a culture of drugs, and the culture of lawless violence ensured that drugs were freely available at every streetcorner.

A college student Imran's father was hurt in a grenade attack in 1992 and went through five major surgeries. In his three years in bed, there was no-one to feed the family. Imran's uncle suffered a psychiatric breakdown and has still not recovered. Another student recalls that her entire family was dragged out of their home on the charge that they fed and harboured terrorists. She was a child then and saw that a badly wounded man covered in blood from head to toe was dragged out of a jeep and asked to identify them as a family that gave them shelter. The critically wounded man insisted that they were strangers and they beat him on his head with rifle butts.

Parents of means sent their children out of Kashmir, so that they could study safely. There they would observe the carefree life of college youth with envy and consternation and realise wistfully how much they had lost. 'Other kids would talk of girls, weekend getaways and discotheques; our life was about escaping bombs and crackdowns.' But after the Gujarat carnage of 2002, many parents feared for their safety in other parts of India and recalled them.

It was not possible for poorer parents to send their children out of Kashmir, and they simply dropped out of school. Their fathers and elder brothers would either be picked up for long periods, or were too frightened to go out for work, so there was no money to pay for their school fees or books. Mothers would also ask children to drop out of school because there were grenades and gunfire every other day. Shafi said that he walked eight kilometres to school, but school was open on an average of just two days a week. The rest of the days, there were strikes or crackdowns. His mother felt he was safer at home. He soon started adding to his mother's earnings by working as an apprentice tailor. 'There were nights when we had to beg our neighbours for food. In times like this, studies are furthest from one's mind,' recalls Shafi. 'I topped Class 12 exams in science. I was interested in bio-technology. Instead, I am weaving shawls.' 'Life is long,' I try to comfort him. But he counters: 'There is still no light visible to these dark times.'

Young people in a water-locked slum in the middle of Dal Lake in Srinagar said they were often picked up only because they could not speak any language except Kashmiri, and security men misunderstood their answers. They felt bitterly trapped. The violence had anyway almost extinguished their livelihood as tourism and trade were in shambles. No one could study: the slum does not have a single graduate today. At night, escaping armed militants would arrive in shadowy, silent *shikaras* and stop over in their homes, demanding food, money and a place to rest. They had no option except to concede, or to lose their lives. The next morning, the army or CRPF would be in their homes, thrashing and arresting them for harbouring militants. It is customary to stock their homes with grain when it is cheap, but the soldiers would see their filled stores and insist that this was to feed the militants.

A young college postgraduate speaks with the controlled and deceptively calm rage of someone twice her age, 'My father was an engineer, but he was killed, and the papers the next day carried the claim of the army that he was a Hibz commander. But it is not just my father I mourn. Every person they kill is my father, my brother, my son.'

These young people, unlike their elders, have never known what 'peace' is. They identify India with the army and paramilitary forces. Their worldview is overshadowed by their experience of the deaths, destruction and degradation that have marked their lives. Treated with insolence and suspicion, robbed of their dignity and humanity, they are not afraid of guns and proudly proclaim their readiness to make the 'supreme sacrifice' of dying for the cause. They shout slogans like 'We want freedom, Go India, go back', scribble graffiti like 'Burhan is our hero' and, when confronted by security forces, they don't hesitate to pick up stones and hurl them at their assailants, knowing well that they could be killed or jailed for that gesture of defiance.

Jha says, 'The older half of this generation have families, enterprises, jobs and aspirations, and are therefore prepared to moderate their political demands in the pursuit of peace. But it is the younger, highly impressionable half—those who are under 20 and have not yet developed any stake in stability—that are the most volatile. This is the generation whom the policy of repression first, dialogue later, has all but lost.'[15]

He explains: 'For the police's endless hunt for "terrorists" has made the life of anyone who has ever hurled a stone in a moment of rage, a living hell. Once arrested and "history-sheeted", or simply caught on video, young people lose their civic rights and become the first targets of every subsequent police inquiry, interrogation or crackdown. Never knowing when this will happen next has frazzled their nerves till almost any fate has become preferable to continuing to live in this uncertain hell. In all of us, frazzled nerves lead to increasingly frequent outbursts of anger. It is only when a 12-year-old boy is tear-gassed or sprayed with pellets, arrested and jailed, that the spasm of anger that made him pick up a stone congeals into hatred, and another insurgent is born.'[16]

During our visit to the valley in the melancholy winter of 2016 we met several young men and women who claimed that they were ready to give up their lives for the freedom of Kashmir. Have they really lost the fear of death? It is difficult to say. But the fact that a large number of young men, and now increasingly women too, come out on the streets raising slogans for *azadi* and confronting the Indian security forces knowing well the brute consequences, is a sign of their implacable resoluteness. The ongoing collective resistance, apparently without any supporting organisation, is

---

15 Jha, 'For Kashmir's Future'.

16 Ibid.

a new form of the old Kashmiri tradition called *Hal Sharee* (helping each other on a voluntary basis) without having any organisational system. In the past, many issues in Kashmir have been settled through the process of *Hal Sharee*. The collective resistance that we are seeing today, is evidence that this system has now evolved into community participation whereby communities are coming together to participate in the process of resolving the political conflict. While the Indian state had earlier been able to condemn the struggle in Kashmir as being 'part of Pakistan's proxy war against India', it is increasingly delusional or disingenuous, or both, to deny the more local roots of the present insurgency.

Even if Kashmiri youth are not flocking to militant groups as they did in the early 1990s, the use of violence to address grievance, perceived or real, is gaining popularity, although with a much smaller number of persons than in the past. Unlike those who took up arms in the early 1990s, the new militants are educated, employed, well-to-do, tech-savvy, and active on social media. Hizbul Mujahedeen's Mohammad Ishaq Parray, also known as 'Newton', who was killed in March 2016, was at the top of his class, scoring 98.4 per cent marks in his Class 10 exams. A few months earlier, Zakir Rashid Bhat, also from the Hizbul Mujahedeen, was killed by the security forces. He was a civil engineering student in Chandigarh before joining the group in March 2015.

The new militants flaunt their identity online. A photograph of a group of 11 uploaded on Facebook shows them with their faces uncovered and their weapons on display. Such audaciousness seems to have excited many of their cohorts. According to reports, the number of local youths joining the militants has more than doubled over the last couple of years. According to police records, 31 local youths joined the militant group in 2013. The number for 2015, even with figures only until the end of September 2016, stood at 66. In 2013, an intelligence assessment estimated that the ratio of local-to-foreign militants stood at 40 local boys to 60 from outside. In 2015, this was reversed to 60:40.

Burhan Wani, whose assassination triggered the latest round of violence, belonged to this new generation of militants. Audio clips of his speeches have become a rage among Kashmiri youth. It is said that several young men from South Kashmir were motivated to take up arms by Burhan's speeches. *The Guardian* observes, 'Wani was a new breed of militant: unlike the first generation of Kashmir separatist fighters in the early 1990s, he did not cross over into Pakistan; he didn't use a *nom de guerre*, and he amassed a huge following on social media, where he issued brazen challenges to the Indian state. It was therefore no surprise that thousands attended Wani's funeral in his hometown of Tral – or that those who could not get there organised their own funeral services across the Kashmir valley.'[17]

The return of popular support for militancy is often explained by security analysts as Pakistan's new strategy of recruiting local Kashmiris and providing them with rudimentary training. Such an analysis fails to take into account the intensity of anger among the people of Kashmir today. The decision by the People's Democratic Party (PDP), a Kashmiri party, to partner the BJP in forming the J&K state government after the 2014 elections, has also caused widespread dismay among PDP's core supporters. Many of the people we met in the Valley expressed their feeling of betrayal on learning about this politically expedient alliance, particularly since, during the election campaign, Mufti himself had urged voters who did not want to vote for the PDP to opt for the National Conference or Congress, rather than the BJP.

The growing trend of ignoring curfews and other restrictions on movements and assembly in public places, the fact that large numbers flock to the funerals of assassinated militants and protests even before guns trained to kill, are clear signs of a growing popular defiance. The hurling of stones and bricks at security personnel, who have demonstrated their alacrity in pumping bullets and pellets into crowds at close range, is gaining traction among the protesting youth. In fact, the extended spell of protests following the killing of Burhan Wani signals a mounting alienation from the Indian state in the Valley, and a loss of faith in the usefulness of democracy and dialogue in altering the harsh reality.

17 Mirza Waheed, 'India's Crackdown in Kashmir: Is This the World's First Mass Blinding?' *The Guardian*, 8 November 2016.

We as Indian citizens need to be aware that when this new generation of Kashmiris seeks *azadi*, it is a constant reminder of the failure, not just of the Indian state, but civil society in the country to stand up and speak out in favour of the legitimate rights of the Kashmiris. They will remember how we failed them.

An 'Epidemic of Dead Eyes'[18]

The bloody months of stone-throwing mass agitations in the Kashmir valley in 2016 left in their wake what has come to be known as the 'epidemic of dead eyes'. Despite widespread dismay and criticism of the use of pellet guns against agitating crowds because these blinded hundreds of children and youth, the government made it clear in 2017 that its forces would continue to deploy these in Kashmir. Close on the heels of these ominous warnings made by the army chief, the Director General of the Central Reserve Police Force K. Durga Prasad, announced the government's resolve to continue to use pellet guns against protesting civilians in the valley, although with some modifications to reduce injuries to the face and eyes. The only concession to outraged public sentiment was an assurance that the guns would be fitted with a deflector to reduce, but not eliminate, chances of the pellets hitting the face and eyes or sensitive organs in the abdomen. But these safeguards would depend on the soldier in fact adhering to protocols of firing at the feet of the agitators. And even if he does, since each round of pellet gunfire would release a spray of hundreds of pellets, there is no guarantee that these will not blind or disable people, mostly young people, but also women in the crowds and bystanders. Small children watching from windows have been blinded by pellets. These proclamations signalled clearly that there would be no change in the current government's muscular Kashmir policy.

According to reports, 972 eye surgeries were carried out by doctors in various hospitals. A senior eye surgeon told us that 570 persons suffered ruptures in their eyeballs due to pellet injuries. It is feared that several of

---

18 A term first used in NYT: https://www.nytimes.com/2016/08/29/world/asia/pellet-guns-used-in-kashmir-protests-cause-dead-eyes-epidemic.html

these people might lose their eyesight. Eighty per cent of the injured are below 25 years of age. They are schoolgoing minors, college students, and young professionals. The situation was described by the *New York Times* as the 'An Epidemic of "Dead Eyes" in Kashmir'.[19]

The *Guardian* reports, 'In a matter of four to five weeks this summer, Indian troops, with a clear mandate to be unsparing, wounded over 10,000 people. One of the youngest, five-year-old Zohra, was admitted to a hospital in Srinagar with lacerations to her abdomen and legs. Fourteen-year-old Insha was in the family kitchen when a swarm of pellets pierced her face. She has lost vision in both eyes. In southern Kashmir, four girls, aged between 13 and 18, were shot in their faces last week. The prognosis for the youngest of these, 13-year-old Ifra Jan, 'is not good', a doctor said. It is doubtful that these little girls posed a threat to the military force, estimated at 700,000 soldiers and police, stationed in Kashmir.'[20]

Nowhere in the world are steel pellets used on crowds. Even Israel does not fire steel pellets on protesting Palestinians. E.N. Rammohan, former BSF Director General who has served in Kashmir, has said that pellets were never used in Kashmir during the time he served there, 'This is very wrong. Many of those who suffered pellet injuries are becoming blind. Seeing them, another thousand will pick up guns.'

Many countries have banned the police from using ammunition meant for hunting animals. The multidirectional spray of pellets was designed to catch prey in flight. Yet several countries continue to use these metal pellets as a means to control civilian demonstrators. In Israel, security forces often deploy lethal and 'non-lethal' ammunition against Palestinian protesters, and crowd-control weapons have blinded at least five young Palestinians in the last two years. In 2011, months after the uprising in Tahrir Square that toppled an Egyptian dictator, a young police lieutenant, Mohamed el-Shenawy, became infamous for firing pellets into the eyes of protesters against Egypt's

---

19 https://www.nytimes.com/2016/08/29/world/asia/pellet-guns-used-in-kashmir-protests-cause-dead-eyes-epidemic.html

20 Waheed, 'India's Crackdown in Kashmir'.

military government. His exemplary skill at blinding civilians earned him the nickname the 'eye sniper', and his notoriety as a symbol of ongoing state brutality eventually led to a three-year jail sentence. The use of rubber bullets by police was banned in the Spanish region of Catalonia in 2014, after at least seven people were blinded by them on the streets of Barcelona.[21]

To date the government of India continues with the policy of using massive force despite claiming that it has asked its forces to use 'maximum restraint'. While explaining its position on the use of pellets, a spokesperson for the government of Jammu and Kashmir had told the media: 'We disapprove of it .... But we will have to persist with this necessary evil till we find a non-lethal alternative.'[22]

Expressing serious concern over violent protests in Jammu and Kashmir in 2010, Prime Minister Manmohan Singh in August 2010 had called for revisiting standard operating procedures and 'non-lethal, yet effective and more focussed' crowd-control measures to deal with public agitations. He had asked Home Minister P. Chidambaram to establish a high-powered task force to come out with a set of recommendations over the next two to three months on non-lethal crowd-control measures. The recommendations of the committee are still awaited.

No one in the central government or the armed forces till date have expressed any regrets about the blinding of children. It seems that the Indian state had decided that blinding a few hundred young Kashmiris was necessary for keeping Kashmir in check. It is inexplicable why photos of the pellet-riddled, pock-marked faces and torsoes of young girls and boys have not moved the Indian media. In any other country it would have raised an uproar.

In any democratic country, the fundamental principle that must govern lawful crowd dispersal is the minimum necessary application of force. The force that is used against violent crowds should be unavoidable and proportionate to the violent actions of the crowd. It should be carefully

---

21 Adil Akhzer, 'What are Pellet Guns and Why are they so Lethal?', *The Indian Express*, 22 July 2016.

22 Ibid.

calibrated, targeted and deliberate. Deadly force should be used as only the last resort, after all other measures are tried and have failed, and after due warning to the crowd. Even when this last-resort lethal force is used, it should be a deterrent rather than retributive, and should be followed by full medical attention to save the life and limb of the injured person.

None of these standards are met by pellet guns, therefore these are very rarely used against civilian populations anywhere else in the world. Every time the pellet guns are fired, these spray 500–700 pellets. It is impossible for the pellets to accurately target a particular individual or the most violent sections of the mob, therefore the random hitting of innocent bystanders is highly probable. Pellets are made of lead, and are irregular in shape, and their rough edges cause unpredictable damage when they hit sensitive parts of the body. Pellets are particularly destructive when they enter the eye. The soft tissue of the retina is irreparably destroyed by the trauma of high-velocity lead pellets. Doctors in hospitals in Srinagar worked heroically almost without sleep for several weeks to try to save the eyes of hundreds of young patients in 2016. Often the lead pellets got embedded so deeply in the skull that doctors could not extract them. The pellets could then lead to poisoning and unpredictable disasters later in the patient's life. Bullets kill, but pellets leave them blinded or disabled for a lifetime. And many patients did not approach a government hospital for treatment for fear that merely having pellet injuries could mark you as a stone-pelter and the police would immediately register criminal charges against you.

The instrument of violence deployed by the masses of Kashmir's youthful agitators is stones. The answer of the Indian security establishment to their stones is bullets and pellet guns. Despite the fact that pellet guns fail to meet any standards of national and international law for crowd control, the government's continued defiant deployment of pellet guns, and the army chief's muscular warnings of 'tough action' against even those who do not use the gun, are deeply troubling. Commandant Chaudhary tells the *New York Times* that he sometimes faces crowds of more than 1,000 hostile young men with a contingent of 20 or 30. The pellet gun, he says, 'is by far the most effective weapon at his disposal. It causes bodily injury, so you will be feared.'

His battalion commander, Rajesh Yadav, nods in agreement. 'If you pinch them, only then people will understand.'

Even more troubling is the response of the highest court of justice in India to this question. On 28 March 2017, during the fourth hearing of the J&K Bar Association's appeal for banning the use of pellet guns in the valley, the Supreme Court apparently told the Bar Association that it would ask the Central government to stop using pellet guns if the Bar Association was able to persuade the Kashmiri youth to stop pelting stones and return to schools and colleges. 'We can direct them (the government) to suspend use of pellet guns for two weeks, but you must assure that violence and stone pelting will stop,' said the Chief Justice of India, J.S. Khehar. Earlier the Attorney General had insisted that the Bar Association must first come up with a solution that would get the youth off the streets.

This was an odd response to the plea of a people who are being blinded and killed by a weapon which is not used anywhere else in the country for mob control. The Bar is asking the Supreme Court to look at the disproportionate use of force by the government and the massive damage that this so-called non-lethal weapon has caused to the people of Kashmir. The plea is also pointing out that the security forces are using a weapon about which it has very little information. In the High Court of Jammu and Kashmir, the CRPF admitted that it had fired nearly 1.3 *million* pellets at protesters in Kashmir over a period of 32 days. It also admitted that there was no way to predict how the pellets would spread once it was fired. The CRPF accepted that the pellets could also hit bystanders. Though the government has been talking about replacing the metal pellets with less lethal munitions, there has been little progress on that front. In fact, the government seems to be inclined to continue to use these weapons. In the month of March 2017, the government increased the number of pellet guns in the valley to 5,000. These guns are capable of firing more than 3 million pellets at one go. According to doctors, the type of pellets that have been recovered in Kashmir indicate that the CRPF are using bare metal pellets.

The question which should have engaged the Supreme Court is whether the government forces should use pellet guns? Is this weapon legal? Has its use in crowd control been approved by the Bureau of Police Research and Development (BPRD)? What are the Standard Operating Procedures for using pellet guns in crowd control? And more importantly, how and when was the use of pellet guns by the CRPF approved, particularly as this is not included in the list of 'non-lethal' weapons for the police force of the states?

The *Guardian* reports that in 2016, the International Network of Civil Liberties Organisations and Physicians for Human Rights published a report titled 'Lethal in Disguise'. 'Pellet rounds,' it stated, 'cause an indiscriminate spray of ammunition that spreads widely and cannot be aimed....' They, therefore, 'are not only likely to be lethal at close range, but are likely to be inaccurate and indiscriminate at longer ranges, even those recommended by manufacturers for safety.'

The other critical legal questions are whether the use of pellet guns conform to Principle 4 of the Code of Conduct of Police in India, which says that as far as practicable, the methods of persuasion, advice and warning should be used. Section 130 of the Code of Criminal Procedure, 1973 (CrPC) clearly states that if the use of force becomes unavoidable, only then should the irreducible minimum force required in the circumstances be used.

It is strange that the Supreme Court, instead of going into the issues of the law, rules and regulations regarding use of force during crowd control, seemed to suggest that it might order the government to stop using pellet guns if the Bar Association could get the youth to stop throwing stones at the security forces.

This response of the Supreme Court to the plea of the J&K Bar Association is radically different from the manner in which it treated the plea of the Extra Judicial Execution Victims' Families Association of Manipur (EEVFAM). In its order at that time, the court had noted that if members of the armed forces are deployed and employed to kill citizens of the country on the mere allegation or suspicion that they are the 'enemy', then not only the rule of law but also democracy would be in grave danger. It said that the use of excessive force or retaliatory force by the Manipur police or the armed forces of the Union is not permissible. It its order the court had directed that the Indian army and other paramilitary forces cannot use 'excessive and retaliatory force' in Manipur and that all allegations of such excessive use of force must be probed.

One wonders why this difference in dealing with the issue of use of excessive force by the state in this case. While the Supreme Court has sent the J&K Bar Association back to Kashmir to talk to the leaders of the agitating people of Kashmir, the government has also told the court that it was not interested in talking to the agitators and their leaders. The Attorney General said 'the court cannot direct the government to meet separatist leaders'.

The government says that it would talk with only 'legitimate' political parties. The point is that the so-called 'legitimate' political parties are not a part of the protest movement. They are a part of the Indian 'mainstream'. They contest elections, form governments and rule over the people of Kashmir. Talking to them is talking to your own side.

Maybe we can say that the government is indeed dialoguing with the protesting groups in Kashmir. But it is not conducting this dialogue through words. It is conducting this dialogue through guns. This is the reality of the government's attitude towards the agitation of the people of Kashmir. The choice of the pellet gun fits in with such a reality.

The *Guardian* asks: is this the world's first mass blinding? 'One of the largest military forces on the planet could not be waging a war against seeing.' 'There is no recorded instance of a modern democracy', it adds, 'systematically and willfully shooting at people to blind them.'

The Human Shield

On 9 April 2017, a 26-year-old shawl weaver, Dar, was one of the few who challenged the militant call for election boycott and left the safety of his home to vote in the by-election for the Srinagar-Budgam parliamentary constituency. Later that morning, Dar was riding his bike to attend a condolence meeting when he was picked up by the army. He told the *Wire* that he was stopped by the forces a few kilometres before Gampora village, where some women were protesting against the elections. 'They damaged my bike, thrashed me severely with gun butts and wooden sticks and in an almost unconscious state tied me to the front of the jeep and paraded me through 10 to 20 villages.' A video shows him tied to the bonnet of the moving army jeep followed by an anti-mine vehicle and a bus with soldiers. 'There was no stone-pelting going on in the area when the army men picked me up and neither did any stone-pelting take place on the [army] vehicles when I was being paraded,' Dar told *The Wire,* adding 'I have never ever in my life hurled stones on forces. But I am not able to understand why I was beaten ruthlessly and then tied to the vehicle. What was my crime? I thought all my bones have been broken as my entire body was in pain due to the ruthless beating. I was in shock, not able to understand what do to as the forces kept threatening me in case I spoke to anybody moving on the road. I was pleading with them to let me go, but they wouldn't listen.' He was first taken to a CRPF camp and then to a local army unit.[23]

In deploying an unarmed citizen, the Indian Army crossed a red line, resorting to a strategy that even the Israeli army avoids. The *Indian Express* reports that even the Supreme Court in Israel has banned the use of human shields. 'In February 2007, AP TV released footage of a 24-year-old Palestinian, Samch Amira, being used as a human shield by Israeli soldiers in Nablus, also in the West Bank. The Israeli Army, after an investigation, suspended the commander whose unit was involved in the act. Then, in 2010, the Israeli Defence Forces prosecuted and convicted two staff sergeants for using civilians as human shields, and handed them 18-month sentences---which HRW criticised for being "excessively lenient"'.[24]

As Siddharth Varadarajan observes, the use of a civilian as a hostage, or 'human shield', was a violation of the right to life and liberty enshrined in the Indian constitution. It was also a violation of international law, since India is a party to the Geneva Conventions of 1949, which prohibits the targeting of civilians in conflicts that are 'not of an international character.'[25]

Despite widespread criticism, the Chief of Army Staff General Bipin Rawat

23 https://thewire.in/124465/kashmir-farooq-ahmad-dar-army/

24 Aakash Joshi, 'Human Shields Everywhere', *The Indian Express*, 26 May 2017.

25 http://www.business-standard.com/article/current-affairs/gogoi-s-kashmiri-human-shield-to-jadhav-why-international-laws-matters-117052300153_1.html

conspicuously awarded Major Leetul Gogoi, the officer who tied Dar to the bonnet, with a Chief of Army Staff Commendation Card for 'sustained efforts in Counter-insurgency operations'. Sources in the army told NDTV that these operations include the use of a local as a 'human shield'. The BJP spokesperson Rao averred, 'Everyone talks about the human rights of terrorists, separatists and disruptive elements. It is high time everyone realize that the security forces, fighting in tough conditions braving all odds, are also humans and have human rights. They have been highly professional and restrained even in some highly provocative situations.'[26] Paresh Rawal, BJP MP, tweeted that he wished to see writer and outspoken critic of the government's human rights record in Kashmir, Arundhati Roy, used as a human shield in Kashmir.[27] He later complained that the Twitter management had bullied him into withdrawing his tweet. Shivam Vij observed, 'So Rawal thinks it's patriotic to invite such violence against people. This is the new normal in an India where lynching is as common as outrage on Twitter.' 'The question nobody will ask', he goes on, 'is why India needs the army, and the army needs to use human shields, against what it calls its own people? What can we do to change the situation? It must be a lot of people pelting stones, and doing so with great ferocity, that one of the world's largest armies needs to take the extreme and unlawful measure of using human shield.'[28]

In an interview, Army Chief General Bipin Rawat defended and praised Major Nitin Leetul Gogoi's action as a warning to stone-pelters. As the *Indian Express* observed editorially, 'By doing this, and by his implied support for the short-circuiting of the army's internal due process vis a vis Major Gogoi's actions—the army commended the major even as a court of inquiry was finalising its probe into the incident—General Rawat risks hurting the enormous institutional credibility of the force that he heads. It bears

26 'Attacks on India's minority Muslims by Hindu vigilantes mount' in *USA Today*, 5 May 2017

27 http://indianexpress.com/article/india/officer-who-tied-kashmiri-man-to-jeep-gets-award-bjp-mp-paresh-rawal-says-do-this-to-arundhati-roy-4669043/

28 Shivam Vij, 'Actor Paresh Rawal Has Scored A Spectacular Self-Goal Suggesting Writer Arundhati Roy Be Used As A Human Shield', *The Huffington Post*, 22 May 2017.

reiteration that Major Gogoi's conduct was a violation of the constitutional promise of due process, and of the fundamental rights enshrined in the Constitution for every citizen, and that it is the army's duty to uphold both.'[29]

The editorial further comments that, 'the army chief treads even further on dangerous ground' with his statements. He declares, "This is a proxy war and proxy war is a dirty war...You fight a dirty war with innovations." He even suggests that it would have been easier for the armed forces if the protestors were firing weapons instead of throwing stones: "Then I could do what I [want to do]."'[30] In effect, General Rawat said that he wished the protestors used bullets instead of stones so he could kill them, because that is what he wished to do! 'But can he afford to lose sight of a fundamental distinction—between armed militants and civilian protestors?'[31] He even further completely steps out of line by expressing his opposition to engaging the protestors through dialogue. 'Has political initiative not been taken in the past? What was the result, you had Kargil....' As the *Indian Express* editorial puts it, 'As General Rawat's responsibility is to guard the nation's physical frontiers from enemies; it is not to draw red lines for political actors in the system.'[32]

It is intensely troubling that not only are we seeing for the first time in independent India an army chief who while in service is openly expressing his political opinions about how he feels governments should treat Indian citizens, but that his politics are so far to the extreme right. It has to be said, however, that his views reflect the current hard line. No talks if protests continue. Prime Minister Modi, with his inexhaustible fondness for alliteration, asks Kashmiris to choose between tourism and terrorism. The penalty for not choosing 'tourism', he does not add, is the bullet and pellet. 'All these activities of stone-pelting have to stop. Then will the government

---

29 http://indianexpress.com/article/opinion/editorials/general-rushes-in-army-general-bipin-rawat-kashmir-4679921/

30 Ibid.

31 Ibid.

32 Ibid.

consider talking,' said K.S. Dhatwalia, a home ministry spokesman, according to a report by *Reuters*.[33]

SCENES FROM A HOSPITAL WARD

A report in the *Guardian* published on 8 November 2016 commented, 'Hospitals in Kashmir, began to resemble scenes from the great wars of the 20th century. Rows of beds with blindfolded boys and girls on them, parents waiting anxiously, doctors and paramedics in attendance around the clock.' As security forces rained metal pellets upon protesters, bystanders and homebound schoolchildren, the wounded were taken to hospitals by the dozen, like birds in the hunting season. [34]

'Children as young as four and five now have multiple pellets in their retinas, blinding them partially, or fully, for life', says the *Guardian*. At the start of September, doctors at Kashmir's main hospital reported that on average, one person had their eyes ruptured by pellets every other hour since 9 July. 'It means *12 eye surgeries per day*,' one doctor told a local newspaper. 'It is shocking.'[35]

Doctors worked heroically round the clock, every waking hour, for several weeks, trying to save as many eyes as they could. In three days, they operated on more patients than they had in three years.[36] 'We had no medical textbooks to guide us', they told us, 'because pellets have never been used on this scale against civilian populations anywhere in the world.' They would try to relieve the pain, extract the bullet, and save the eye of the patient. But often the eye was beyond repair, and the bullet so deeply embedded in the skull that it was impossible to extract it. They have no clear idea of what the embedded bullet will do to the body, and when. 'It was hardest because most of our patients were children.'

---

33 'Spontaneous Protests Wrongfoot Police, Loosening India's grip on Kashmir', *Reuters/ Firstpost*, 11 May 2017.

34 https://www.theguardian.com/world/2016/nov/08/india-crackdown-in-kashmir-is-this-worlds-first-mass-blinding

35 Waheed, 'India's Crackdown in Kashmir'.

36 Ibid.

Ellen Barry of the *New York Times* describes the scene inside the operation theatres.

> The street outside is patrolled by riot police officers in camouflage, bracing for the nightly spasm of violence, but it is quiet here inside the operating room. The surgeon's knife slides into an eyeball as if it were a soft fruit. The patient's eyelids have been stretched back with a metal clamp, so his eyeball bulges out of glistening pink tissue. The surgeon sits with his back very straight, cutting with tiny movements of his fingers. Every now and then, a thread of blood appears in the patient's eye socket. The patient is 8 years old.
>
> 'Very bad,' murmurs the surgeon, Dr. S. Natarajan. But then, all 13 cases he will see today will be very bad...The patients have mutilated retinas, severed optic nerves, irises seeping out like puddles of ink. 'Dead eyes,' the ophthalmology department's chief calls them.[37]

Mehraj Bhat volunteered for two months in the ophthalmology unit at the Shri Maharaja Hari Singh (SMHS) hospital, Srinagar, Kashmir, and gives a heart-rending account of what he saw there. The Ophthalmology unit, which according to doctors 'used to be a ghost ward before the uprising is now the most busy and fearsome ward in the hospital.' He describes the trauma of the doctors. Dr Raashid Maqoob, working in the SMHS, recorded his agony in a Facebook post, 'When I wanted a break from the emotional scenes inside our theatre, I walked into the next room, trauma theatre of the surgery department with my surgical gown on.... I witnessed the team of surgeons and anaesthetists resuscitating a young 24-year-old bullet-ridden body...the guy lost the battle and he died. I couldn't hold myself and burst into tears.'

Dr Raashid told Bhat, 'Doctors have to take consent from a patient or

---

37 Ellen Barry, 'An Epidemic of "Dead Eyes" in Kashmir as India Uses Pellet Guns on Protesters', *New York Times,* 28 August 2016.

his family before performing surgery but in this situation doctors have been receiving patients who are near-unconscious, blinded or younger than 18 but people bringing them were also most often friends or strangers, not family, so we ended up having to get quick signatures from the kids themselves, while wheeling them into surgery.' Sitting on a bench outside the medical college, another doctor Yaqoub says, 'As doctors we usually feel neutral, we treat the wound, not the person, but when I see this extent of discrimination and heartless violence, I want to shun the neutrality and take sides.' Bhat adds, 'A young Kashmiri himself, Yaqoub grew up in the nineties listening to the same "tales of loss and betrayal" as the youth protesting today.... He says to me, "For some reason, I became a doctor and banked on optimism."'

Even when the patients are being treated in the hospital, policepersons visit the ward to register cases against them as stone-pelters. Many families we met in Kashmir said they had not taken their injured children to public hospitals for fear that the police would charge them with crimes, and their lives would be ruined further. Bhat said no patient files are tied to the hospital beds, as is the practice in all hospitals. Instead they are given numbers.

A senior surgeon who did not want to divulge his identity told Bhat that 'We decided to restrict the files to ourselves because the security agencies come and take the names and address of these patients from the files and start harassing and minting money from them after they are discharged from the hospitals.' One of the attendants, a father in his 60s nursing his 20-year-old bullet-injured son in ward 16 told Bhat, 'I am getting regular calls from the SHO (in-charge of the police station) of my area inquiring about the date of discharge from the hospital.' He adds, 'They shot him in his abdomen and after we tried to bring him to hospital took him out from the ambulance and started hitting his wound with guns which damaged his intestines.' Bhat adds, 'The presence of security agencies in hospitals is psychologically so depressing that a lot of patients don't even visit hospitals for their treatment.'

A citizen fact-finding team also catalogues instances where ambulances and other medical services were allegedly obstructed by security forces, which meant that the injured could not reach hospitals in time. 'For instance, in Choon village, we were told that families were scared to take the wounded to hospitals as the police were making rounds to pick up people. In Karimabad, residents told us that they preferred to wait for a day or two before taking the injured to hospitals. In Baramulla district, villagers avoided using arterial roads to transport pellet and bullet victims and often travelled during night time to avoid being detected.'

The most haunting are the stories that Bhat tells of the young patients themselves. Almost 95 per cent of the patients he saw were targeted above their waists. A majority of them had pellets in their eyes: 'a new generation of young kids maimed and blinded for life at least in one eye.' More than 500 boys lost one eye and more than 30 had bilateral injuries (both eye pellet injuries). The fear of losing the vision has left an impact on their mental health. When Bhat met them, he found that most of the time these young and minors who have been left blind in one or both eyes owing to the pellet injuries, huddle around to talk about the 'tougher days ahead', the 'dark future' and the 'life of a blind'.

Feroz Ahmad, a youth from Sopore, who has pellet injuries in both eyes with minimal chances of him recovering his eyesight tells his friend: 'I want to talk to my mother; she must be worried.... I haven't talked to her for all these days.' But, moments later, he stops his friend from making a call to his home. 'They don't know about my position. Mouj (mother) will be worried for the whole night.... I will talk to them in the morning,' he says as tears continuously roll down his face.

'The scene is filled with emotions again', Bhat reports. 'Fayaz recites verses from the holy Quran, asking his friends to pray for his recovery. There is pin drop silence in the Ward.'

There is also solidarity. 'A youth from the main town of Pulwama, blinded in both eyes due to the pellet injuries, is helped by another youth from Tral, who has lost his vision in one of his eyes, out of the Ward. With arms around each other's shoulders, the two youths come out in the corridor for a walk.'

Gowhar, a 21-year-old, six-feet-tall boy was supposed to get married next month. He was also preparing for next year's heavyweight bodybuilding championship. He had no idea then that he would be hit by pellets in both the eyes which would leave his dreams shattered. Bhat writes, 'While we were consoling him about the loss of his eyes, a man with a white beard and a young girl standing beside him introduced themselves and said something which ended up (leaving) everyone in tears: "I have given my daughter to the boy when he was fine and it would be unethical and immoral if I take a backseat when this tragedy has befallen my would-be son-in-law." His daughter added, "I will marry him on the same date we were supposed to get married whether he regains his eyesight or not."'

But mainly there is despair. Bhat writes, 'Shiraz Ahmad Ahangar, 26, spoke to his mother in Murran (Pulwama) telling her (on the cell phone), "I am hit by pellets. But you don't worry, I am alright." Then, unable to hold his emotions for long, he let out a loud cry and said, "I wish it was a bullet. It hurts...it hurts badly, mother." Everybody around him—a small crowd of friends, well-wishers, local journalists and photographers, other pellet victims—began crying. A friend, who was sitting at the corner of his bed, quickly snatched the phone from his hand and assured his wailing mother "he is alright, just a bit frightened". But everybody around could see that Ahangar was not frightened but in pain, and why not, he has more than hundred pellets in his body.'

II

Pain 'Helter-skelter': The Human Cost of 2016

The period following the assassination of Burhan Wani on 8 July 2016 will go down in the annals of the country as one of the most brutal periods ever witnessed in the Kashmir Valley. It changed the rules of the Indian Army's engagement with the civilian population by adopting mass blinding as strategy, deeming stone-pelters as 'overground workers of terrorists',[38] and normalising new forms of military aggression.

It is impossible to fully account for the human costs of this interregnum. How can blood on the street be calculated in terms of loss? Can a price be attached to the disconsolate grief of a woman beating her head against a wall on hearing of the death of her husband? No media image of a young, pellet-shattered face, gut-wrenching though it may be, can capture the lingering death of a blinded child's future. What can only be said is that this has been a period that has seen a democratic state discard both the laws of humanity and the principles of its constitution in a bid to impose its writ on a people.

A major flashpoint in the unravelling of this tragic script was the manner in which the Indian army chose to respond to the Wani funeral on 11 July 2016, as tens of thousands of mourners defied curfew and converged at the venue of the funeral in Tral. When a section of the mourners protested the

38 Statement of Indian Army Chief Bipin Rawat made on 15 February 2017.

Wani killing by raising slogans against the Indian state and throwing stones at uniformed armed personnel, they were fired upon with live ammunition. The ensuing deaths led to a sharp escalation in public anger, as street clashes quickly spread across the Valley, engulfing both urban and rural areas. It was also for the first time that women and girls participated in the protests in such large numbers. As one eyewitness reported, 'I saw thousands of young girls coming out from their homes, marching towards Burhan's funeral amid slogans in support of Azadi and the militants.'[39] This turning point in public resistance in the Valley was met with a severely repressive response from the Indian state. It is the human costs of this response that we will now consider in this chapter.

There were two important aspects to the repression perpetrated by the Indian state during this period. On the one hand, was the weaponisation of the response; on the other, there was the launching of a war of attrition against the general public in the weeks and months that followed.

Weaponisation of Response

Coming to the first aspect, the wide, indiscriminate and persistent use of pellet guns despite their deadly, and often permanent impact on protestor and bystander alike, indicated the unequivocal intent of the Indian state to inflict crushing costs on an unarmed population. Pellet guns had lethal consequences but the Indian security forces cynically took refuge in the fact that they were classified as 'non-lethal'. In other words, a formal categorisation was allowed to trump the evidence on the grounds that these arms and ammunition were in fact perpetrating unacceptable harm on protestors. As experts had noted, they were 'inherently inaccurate, indiscriminate, and capable of penetrating soft tissue even at a distance'... that they 'should not be used for crowd management or for crowd dispersal, as most of these weapons cannot be used safely or effectively against crowds.'[40]

---

39 Bilal Kuchay, 2016, 'A Hero's Farewell', *Kindle*, 18 July.

40 'Blind to Justice: Excessive Use of Force and Attacks at Health Care in Jammu and Kashmir, India', Physicians for Human Rights, December 2016.

A fact-finding report of the Physicians for Human Rights pointed out that this 12-gauge gun was no 'birdshot' deployed in amateur bird-hunting expeditions but used explosive powers. In addition to its lethal design, the ammunition for this shotgun is the No. 9 shot, which is a lead alloy pellet loaded into cartridges filled with up to 616 pellets, which can penetrate soft tissue when fired even from a distance. 'At shorter distances, the pellets will remain clustered together, and the impact on soft tissue will be concentrated on a smaller area, meaning the ammunition can be lethal to humans at close range.'[41]

In innumerable instances, in order to quell the protests, these guns were used at close range and above the abdomen, contrary to all humanitarian norms and even the SOPs (standard operating procedures) for crowd control of the Indian armed forces. Yet, even as hundreds of grievously injured children were being rushed to hospital during the period immediately following the Wani assassination, both the local police and the army maintained that there could be no compromising on the use of the pellet gun. On 26 July 2016, the Northern Command Chief, General D.S. Hooda, supporting the stand of the Central Reserve Police Force that it would continue to use pellet guns, stated, 'There is a requirement of non-lethal weaponry and pellet guns are classified as part of the non-lethal weaponry.'

Particularly interesting to note here is that while shells containing Pelargonic Acid Vanillylamide (PAVA), a synthetic version of a compound found in chillies, were suggested as less lethal ammunition for crowd control and introduced in September 2016, it was not long before they were found to be ineffectual in deterring protestors. For the security forces, the pellet gun, no matter the extent of the damage it caused, remained the weapon of choice despite rising concern over the resultant human costs.[42]

41 Ibid.

42 'Kashmir unrest: From Pellet Guns to Chilly Shells, the Full Story', *Indian Express*, 3 September 2016.

War of Attrition against People

As for the war of attrition mounted on the population of the Valley, it took on many forms. There were constant attempts, for instance, to prevent protesters from accessing medical aid and medical personnel from reaching the hospitals, which was again a clear violation of international humanitarian law. Police constantly patrolled hospitals, hospital records came under surveillance and ambulances were followed and often fired upon. According to media estimates, within the first seven days of the protests, around 70 ambulances carrying civilians injured in protests came under attack.[43]

During our interactions with the local population in December 2016, we heard many accounts of such obstruction. Farid Parrey (name changed), a 45-year-old resident of Kulgam village, recalled his moments of absolute desperation when security forces fired at the ambulance carrying his 15-year-old son, who was shot in the knee. In Bijbehara, an ambulance driver of a childline service reported how he would constantly come across families with injured members who were too scared to go to the hospital. 'Many cases of delayed treatment and lack of medical expertise have led to infections, deformations, and other complications. We also notice in these families the constant fear and anxiety of being identified by the security forces,' he revealed.

The experience of young Masood Ahmed (name changed), who lives in a south Kashmir village, indicated why such anxiety has become an all-encompassing phenomenon, 'When Burhan Wani was martyred, we came out to protest. The police and CRPF people targeted us and an SHO took out his AK-47 and fired upon us. I got bullets in my arm and abdomen. When I was taken to the hospital, the ambulance came under attack. After some months, we got summons to go to the police station. They had made a case against me, labelling me a militant. I was not even pelting stones but because I had two bullets in my body, they are now targeting me again,' said Ahmed. Fear of arrest, police interrogation and incarceration was the main reason why many of the injured preferred to bear the pain and complications of injuries caused

43 Adil Akhzer, 'Kashmir: 70 Ambulances Damaged during Protests', *Indian Express*, 14 July 2016.

by encounters with the security forces, or seek local help. In one case that came to our attention, even a blacksmith was approached to remove a bullet from the body of a grievously injured man.

Inexplicably, the war of attrition was carried into people's homes. In the village of Churat in south Kashmir, we listened to local villagers as they spoke about the nightmare that life had become. One among them remarked, 'While army crackdowns are episodic, what has become permanent is the state of tension in which we exist. The authorities don't want us to enjoy peace. So schools are burnt down just to prevent us from living a normal life and educate our children.'

The tactics of keeping 'fear on the boil' were many—food stocks were raided, window panes wilfully stoned and transformers fired upon. In its fact-finding report, 'Kashmir, A Paradise Lost?', the Centre for Policy Analysis reported, 'Another new element in measures of repression used by the state armed forces in 2016 was the burning of electricity transformers. This was observed in several districts across the Valley, including Anantnag, Baramulla, Srinagar and Budgam. In other places, two to four transformers were blown up in the middle of the night.... Responding to a question on the number of transformers damaged during the protests, the Jammu and Kashmir Assembly was informed this number stood at 368.'[44]

Apart from transformers, pipes were broken in order to disrupt water supply. One of the families we visited in a small town in Kulgam district had just lost a 21-year-old daughter in the crossfire. A day after the killing, security personnel returned to their home and fired at it. The victim's mother recalled, 'They broke all the panes in the house. We couldn't understand why they did this. No family member among us had pelted stones. So was this merely to add more trauma to what we were already going through, to punish us all over again? And for no reason?'

This strategy of spoliation was extended to routine vandalism during

44 'Kashmir, A Paradise Lost? Report on the Current Situation in Kashmir', Centre for Policy Analysis, 2017

search-and-cordon operations. According to the fact-finding done by an alliance of civil society organisations in 2016 when army crackdowns were imposed on houses in Pulwama district, 'properties were vandalised, cash was looted and even a dog shot dead.' The story was the same in the district of Budgam and Baramulla, with the police barging into homes, breaking furniture, toppling refrigerators, etc. In some areas, 'state armed forces forcibly enter people's homes, destroy household property, pour chilli powder into sacks of food grain and take embers from their kangris and pour them over the stored rice used by families to last through winter.'[45]

Communication blackouts 'in the interest of maintenance of public order' was another dimension of this war of attrition. On 16 July, shortly after the protests at the Wani funeral threatened to assume major proportions, the J&K government imposed a ban on newspapers and blocked cable TV. Although the ban was lifted after three days, a particularly fierce critic of government policy, the *Kashmir Reader*, continued to be banned for the next three months. Similarly, there were long spells when the use of private mobile telephony and internet were banned. Finally, in November, postpaid connections were restored but those dependent on prepaid mobile internet services had to wait until January 2017 for services to be restored. Mid-April saw the authorities make another bid to control young protestors by blocking access to 22 social media sites, including Whatsapp, Facebook and Twitter for over a month. Such arbitrary clampdowns have wreaked havoc on ordinary lives, disrupting educational and livelihood opportunities as well as everyday human interaction.

One young man compared it to being consigned to perpetual darkness, 'They shut down communication every time something serious happens and everybody is left in the dark. The sun is shining in the sky but the days turn dark for us. Isn't accessing information our right?'

---

45 'Why Are People Protesting in Kashmir? A Citizens' Report on the Violation of Democratic Rights in the Kashmir Valley in 2016'.

Grievous Physical Harm

The weaponisation of state response, by perpetrating grievous physical harm on an entire population, has led to the creation of a wasteland of death and depression. Almost everybody in the Valley has a personal story to tell about a relative, friend or colleague, who has been impacted directly by the actions of the police or security forces. Those who have lost family members wrestle with depression and a lingering sense of personal loss. Those who have suffered broken limbs and blinded eyes now confront a blighted future, not just for themselves but for their care-givers.

We were forcibly reminded of this unfolding tragedy when we met family after family in the villages of Kulgam district, full of apple and walnut trees and just as rife with stories of death and destruction. Kulgam, incidentally, was one of the epicentres of the post-Wani assassination violence.

The dead live on with striking clarity in the memories of those they left behind. One young man, his arm and thigh scarred by bullet injuries, remembered how his brother had stepped out of the house on hearing protestors outside, shortly after the Wani assassination, 'His hair was wet. He had just had a bath. Within minutes I was picking up his dead body.'

An elderly man, his eyes cloudy with cataracts, could only weep over the body of his wife who was cruelly caught in the crossfire of an encounter that raged outside their home, 'It happened in front of my eyes. She had left my side just for five minutes and before I could even realise it, she was dead. They shot her in the face. They say stone-pelters are wooed with Rs 500 to hurl stones. My wife was 70 years old. Would she have thrown stones at anyone? Those who have no compassion cannot be the beloved of God. Those soldiers had no compassion.'

In another village a mother lost her 21-year-old daughter while standing over a kitchen fire. Her face crumbles in grief as she relates what happened next: 'I heard a big commotion outside the door and they were carrying the body of my child into the house. When we took her to hospital, the doctor could only write on a slip of paper, "Brought dead".'

If these accounts were painful to listen to, it was the stories of children whose lives are suddenly interrupted that proved the most wrenching. In one home we met three school friends, aged between 14 and 15, all of whom have had brief, brutish encounters with the armed might of the Indian state. Fifteen-year Muzamil (name changed) was brought into the room we were sitting in on crutches, helped by his father, uncle and a local acquaintance. It took three grown men to help this child move from one room to another thanks to bullets that had pulverised his kneecap on the day after the Wani assassination. The boy needs no prompting to recall that fateful morning, 'I was on my way to school on 9 July when I noticed a procession of protestors. They were moving peacefully. No one was throwing stones or anything. It was only when the police began to throw stones at them that the demonstrators started throwing stones back. The shooting then began without warning and I became very scared, clutching at my copy and pen. Before I knew it, I had fallen with a sharp pain in my knee and blood was flowing from my leg.'

Muzamil's father recounts how the boy was found with three bullets in his body and when he took him to the local primary health centre he was asked to take the boy to the district hospital at Kulgam. 'For that I had to hire an ambulance, and security forces even fired on it. I was then directed to a bone hospital where surgery was performed. Today, my son has a missing bone in his knee and will need more surgeries to be able to walk again.' There is stoic resignation in his voice, even as his dreams for his son becoming an engineer are now forgotten. His immediate anxiety is to manage the bedsore on the heel of his son's injured leg. 'Right now my biggest challenge is to ensure that the infection does not spread. It needs a daily dressing that costs Rs 200 each time.'

Seated next to Muzamil was 14-year-old Mehmood (name changed). He too was part of that group of schoolboys caught in the firing, and took a bullet in his head. The bullet, thankfully, has been surgically extracted as can be discerned from the faint, semi-circular line etched on the left side of his head where the sutures once were. Mehmood looked at us from under his long, dark eyelashes, but did not seem to register our presence. The bullet left him paralysed on the left side, and he hasn't spoken a word since the injury. His father, a carpet seller, told us that his son seems to be suffering from a neurological problem, even as his son looked on with a doleful, unseeing gaze. His parents say that once he was a happy-go-lucky boy, but today a veil of silence has fallen over him.

The third child in the room, 14-year-old Iqbal (name changed), had a bullet strike him in the right eye and he remembered having bled a lot from that part of his head. Today he says he can see nothing with that eye. His doctor estimates that there is about 20 per cent vision in that eye and chances of recovery of full vision are extremely bleak. Iqbal had only one question to ask us. 'I want to be a doctor, will I be able to study?' The people in the room rushed to comfort him and assure him that he will be able to achieve his ambition, inshallah, but Iqbal himself was not easily consoled. The prospect of a future without a right eye haunted him.

A consultant ophthalmologist at Srinagar's state-run Shri Maharaja Hari Singh (SMHS) Hospital, Dr Sajad Khanday, has come across many boys like Iqbal. He explained, 'The eye is a delicate organ, comprising the cornea, lens, vitreous fluid, retina and optic nerve. If a foreign body penetrates it by as much as one millimetre, it causes grave injuries. Take the cornea. It is half a millimetre thick. If something penetrates it by more than half a millimetre, it can burst and the eye is permanently damaged. If the optic nerve is affected, then again there is permanent damage.'

Pellets, according to Dr Khanday, are particularly dangerous because they come at a high speed and in clusters. Sometimes pellets get lodged behind the eye and they cannot be retrieved. The treatment in itself is a painful experience. Eye operations, on an average, last for half an hour to two hours, and multiple surgeries may be needed with the consequent risk of complications. Many patients of pellet injuries have had to undergo three to four surgeries to recover somewhat.

The pattern of injuries was distinct this time, according to Dr Khanday. 'We have been noticing such pellet injuries from 2010 onwards, and we would get some three or four patients in the hospital a month. In 2016, this pattern changed dramatically in two ways immediately after the Wani assassination: first, in terms of the sheer numbers of patients with such injuries—they would come in clusters. Second, unlike earlier, the eyes and face seemed to be the primary site of injuries, with some also bearing injuries on their scalp,' he said.

According to Dr Khanday's estimation, around 15,000 people had been injured in some way or the other in the first 150 days of the protests because of firing at the hands of the security forces. Of these, 1,600 people suffered pellet injuries on their faces, with 1,155 of them bearing injuries in their eyes of which 300 were injured in both eyes. That it was the young who were disproportionately affected became very clear from Dr Khanday's data. His hospital, SMHS, had around 1,000 cases in this period, with only about 100 being over the age of 40. In other words, 90 per cent of SMHS pellet injury patients were young adults or children below the age of 14.

What does this really translate into, in terms of the ability to live a normal life? As Dr Khanday put it, 'We were able to salvage some vision in 90 per cent of the cases but 70 per cent of patients were not able to recover fully. They will be disabled for life. Those who have lost one eye are now denied the reserve of an extra eye, should something happen to that functioning eye. They also won't be eligible for any employment that requires good vision. At the same time, those left with one eye are relatively fortunate, when compared to their completely blinded counterparts, because one functioning eye can take care of its own function and at least 20 per cent of the other eye, if treatment is successful. For those who have lost both eyes, the prospects are far more grim.'

If one were to stand back and consider the human costs of being so grossly harmed, almost by government fiat, the entire nightmare of the situation in the Valley comes into view. Not only will a society that is far from economically prosperous now have to bear the burden of the health care of these individuals, the opportunity costs for young people rendered disabled in the prime of their life is immeasurable.

Costs Women Bear

Think, for a moment, of the mother of young Mehmood who cannot even articulate the thoughts going through his head. This is what she told us, 'My son was such a happy, mischievous boy. Today he doesn't speak. It's like my life coming to an end.'

When news of his shooting reached her, she fell unconscious and, for a long time, was not able to hear from one ear. Today, all she wants is for him to be independent. 'We feel very, very helpless. Life has become so difficult that we cannot even concentrate. We don't know what to do. My son can't even go to the toilet on his own. My husband is a daily wage earner. Now either he or I have to be with our son at all times, and this also means that our capacity to earn is being affected.' The hospitalisation and after-care has set this family back by more than Rs 2 lakh, and every day brings more expenses. While the neighbours are helpful and pitch in with what they can, before long even such sources of support will fade away. Typically, there is a lot of solidarity for an affected family within the village and even strangers will lend a shoulder. But, ultimately, it is the family alone that will have to manage, find its own resources and reserves of courage. It is then that the interminable battle to cope begins.

Senior journalist, Freny Manecksha, in her new book, *Behold, I Shine*, pointed to the common assumption that women in Kashmir do not bear the brunt of direct violence as the men do, and argued that women's suffering always tends to be underestimated because their stories are difficult to access. And what about the 'indirect violence that is inflicted on them... shouldn't that be accounted for?'[46]

The post-Wani period saw the demolition of the dividing line between direct and indirect violence that women faced since there was a conspicuous spike in their participation in the protests. The team representing the People's Union of Civil Liberties specifically noted after visiting the Valley in October 2016 that 'For the first time in Kashmir as many as six women were killed and several injured. Perhaps for the first time all-women public protests (*juloos*) and the participation of women in *janazas* (funeral processions) in large numbers was observed. Young women were very vocal and said that too much bloodshed had happened and that there could be no compromise this time.'[47] Visuals of girls in school uniforms throwing stones at the security forces that appeared in the national press in recent times only confirmed this reality.

46 Freny Manecksha, 2017, *Behold, I Shine*, New Delhi.

47 Press statement on PUCL National Team's Visit to Kashmir Valley, 2016.

A female college student from Bijbehara, with whom we had a conversation, drew on her own example to explain the new mood among young women like her. 'When we see so much violence being done to us, we are curious to learn about militancy. We read books and newspapers and have learnt about the torture centres and the constant attacks on people. So I asked myself, "Why did Burhan Wani leave home?" The answer, I figured out, was that he left to join the militants because nobody seemed to be taking an interest in solving our issue. The more force you use, the more the anger will grow and more young people will leave their homes and join the ranks of the militants. Boys —and don't be surprised, girls too,' she said.

The new confidence that comes through in these words is striking, but there can be no getting away from the fact that in conflict situations it is women who invariably play the highest price, in terms of both physical harassment and disproportionate burden. Sexual harassment is an ever-present threat because the female body has unfortunately come to symbolise the honour of the community. The noted Sri Lankan human rights activist and academic, Radhika Coomaraswamy, once put it this way, 'Since women's sexuality is seen as being under the protection of the men of the community, its defilement is an act of domination asserting power over the males of the other community or group that is under attack.'[48] Reports of sexual harassment are difficult to access, given the great stigma attached to it. But what is far more visible everywhere is the disproportionate burden women bear in keeping some normalcy within the family going even in challenging circumstances. As we saw in the case of Mehmood's mother, women as primary caregivers often have to act as crutches to grown men even if their own frames are ill-equipped for the task.

It is only while speaking woman-to-woman to the female members of households that these domestic tragedies spill out of otherwise tightly secured reservoirs. Putting food on the table and earning a few rupees through *mazdoori* has now become a particularly arduous task for many

---

48 Radhika Coomaraswamy, 1999: 'A Question of Honour: Women, Ethnicity and Armed Conflict', Third Minority Rights Lecture, Geneva.

women in the villages we visited, because of the added responsibility of looking after those affected by the violence. As usually happens, the lion's share of the family meal is made available to the men and boys of the household, while mothers scrimp and save when it comes to their own consumption. In the process, once blooming cheeks hollow out, cheekbones begin to stand out in gaunt faces and the hair under the hijab grows grey. A young woman school counsellor we met at Bijebehara, noted how the unrest after 8 July has been affecting the mental health of children everywhere and is turning into a worry for their parents, especially mothers. 'Speaking for myself, my own two-and-a-half year-old has learnt to lisp, "azaadi". Our children go to school but don't want to study. Most of those affected are adolescents, and mothers report that aggression in them is rising. They also constantly worry that their children will be caught for pelting stones or go off and join the militants.'

Mental Health Concerns

Dr Arshad Hussain, professor of Psychiatry, Institute of Mental Health & Neurosciences (IMHANS), Srinagar, has been observing the mental health of the general population in the Valley in a situation of conflict from the early 1990s, when he was just a medical student. 'In the old days, there were many stories of distress. I remember, for instance, a young man who would climb a particular tree every morning and sit on it all day. He did this for 20 years before psychiatrists could rehabilitate him.'

It is thanks to the efforts of people like Dr Hussain and civil society organisations that took upon themselves the task of addressing the forgotten issue of psychiatric stress that Kashmir today has both medical expertise and rising awareness. Today mental health is a well-recognised condition and J&K has about 40 trained psychiatrists, unlike three decades ago when people had to depend on family elders, local *pirs* and visits to shrines and dargahs to cope with their mental agony.

Speaking to Dr Hussain provided us with an insight into how large a toll the current violence is taking on the mental health of the population, a trend that was perceptible in the outpatient department of IMHANS, which gets around 150 patients, coming in from all parts of the Valley, every day.

According to his estimation, at least 11 per cent of the population suffer from mental health morbidity currently.

Dr Hussain pointed out that trauma is the result of an abnormal event in the natural cycle of life; there were two aspects to recovering from such trauma: gaining a feeling of internal security and a feeling of external security. Both these are difficult to achieve in situations of constant violence. Typically, people will somehow manage. Belief systems evolved, fathers grew more pious, neighbours extended a hand of support, but the families of those left permanently disabled will never be able to escape the perpetual cycle of struggling to cope. According to Dr Hussain, while death brings intense grief and suffering, there was also closure. But here, as in cases of disappearances, the trauma was unending. In all cases of such loss, there were also secondary traumas within the family like financial breakdowns because of the loss of an earning member or a job. Unemployment is a major trigger factor for mental health disorders in the Valley, with unemployed persons having twice the possibility of going into clinical depression than their employed counterparts. Also, the poorer the person was, the higher the trauma of the adverse events they experienced.

In the immediate aftermath of the Wani assassination, there was a widespread feeling of insecurity among the general population, according to Dr Hussain, something that was last perceived in the early 1990s when there was the midnight knock syndrome, with patients getting panic attacks at night as they kept imagining people coming in search of them. This time, however, there was a significant change. Because the use of force was much more widespread and had permeated every section of society, there was more anger and less fear. 'You now have a generation that is desensitised to fear,' observed Dr Hussain.

What also come out clearly in the data is that women were twice as likely to suffer mental health morbidity than men. Among the cases that came to Dr Hussain's attention over the years was a woman who was so affected by her son's death that she banged her head in despair and fractured her skull. Another shattered mother would visit shrines and keep repeating the words, 'Get my son.' This morbidity may be noticed by the rest of the family, but most often it is just accepted as a normal physical change. One of Dr Hussain's patients began losing her eyesight after she learnt of her son's death. Family members thought it was related to age. Yet, as Dr Hussain pointed out, trauma did have physiological impacts as well. This was clearly the case with Mehmood's mother as well, when she mentioned that she had lost hearing in one ear from the moment she heard of her son's injury.

Interestingly, women not only bear the burden of reversals within the family, they contribute towards stemming what Dr Hussain pointed out as 'social drift', when a family member becomes socially dysfunctional. They were also the ones who observed changes in family members and invariably took the lead in bringing affected people to hospital, either as mothers, sisters or wives. As he put it, 'Women we find constitute the largest group of survivors. They demonstrate a higher resilience in terms of coping. They are the ones who tend to see the brighter side of things, telling victims "at least you are alive!".'

But hope, 'that thing with feathers/That perches in the soul' as the poet Emily Dickinson wrote so long ago—is difficult to hold on to in the Kashmir Valley today. The ordeals and uncertainties marking life formed a constant thread in the conversations we had with Kashmiris across age-groups and backgrounds. What was most conspicuous in these conversations was the death of hope—hope that the violence will abate, hope that life would become more secure, hope that a modicum of justice would be delivered, hope that the Indian state was serious about addressing the Kashmir issue.

As Professor of International Law, Sheikh Shaukat Hussain, observed, 'We have been engaged in so many exercises for dialogue. Over the years we have been telling and re-telling our accounts to anyone who will listen, knowing full well that nothing will emanate from these conversations. There is a sort of hopelessness we feel when we search for any remedy within your system.'

The irony of the Government of India claiming Kashmir as part of its country, yet treating it in ways markedly different, is not lost on Kashmiris. 'They want Kashmir, the land; not Kashmiris, the people', was an observation we heard again and again. It startled us to hear young Amir, still nursing a wound caused by a pellet gun in July, whisper, 'After they cause such wounds, no one from the government even bothers to come and ask about our condition. They hate us, they want to remove us from the face of the earth.'

The questions put to us had no answers. How was it that if suo moto action could be taken by the courts in the case of the Bhagalpur blindings in Bihar, no one bothers when hundreds of people suffer blindings from the use of pellet guns in the Valley? Why is it that pellet guns are not used to quell protests when Jats go on a rampage, as they did in March 2016, or in the instance of angry mobs burning buses in Karnataka in September 2016? What is the reason that the Supreme Court of India took cognisance of the excessive use of force by the state in Manipur, but refused to rule against the use of pellet guns in Kashmir unless it can be guaranteed that stone pelting would end?

Like the threads woven into the exquisite shawls the Valley produces, questions arise, twine and intertwine, creating a narrative of their own—a narrative of a fissured earth.

III

What Came Before The Beginning: First India-Pakistan War

The conflict in Kashmir started soon after British India was divided into the independent states of India and Pakistan. The process of this partition displaced between 10 and 12 million people along religious lines accompanied by large-scale violence with estimates of loss of life varying between several hundred thousand and two million.

Jammu and Kashmir was a princely State under British suzerainty. There were 584 princely states scattered all over the subcontinent, covering about 45 per cent of its surface with a total population of about 99 million. The relations between the princely states and the British were based on treaties with the British Crown, the paramount power controlling their foreign relations and defence. The princes were guaranteed their right of succession and autonomy in internal affairs. The British, at the time of their departure, had made it clear to the rulers of these princely states that they had no independent future and they must accede to one of the two newly emerged dominions—India and Pakistan. The British had also encouraged the rulers of these princely states to consider geographical factors and the will of their subjects in deciding accession. There was no demand for partition of any of the princely states, while the rest of the subcontinent was being partitioned on communal lines.

Like all other princely states, after the transfer of power, Jammu and Kashmir was expected to accede to either of the two dominions, India or

Pakistan. According to the 1941 Census, nearly 77 per cent of Jammu and Kashmir's population was Muslim. At the time of Partition, Jammu and Kashmir's major geographical communications, and economic links were with the areas of Western Punjab and the North West Frontier Province which were to be part of Pakistan. The only railway line that entered the princely state was from Sialkot, located about 30 km inside the territory of west Punjab which was to be part of Pakistan. Of the three roads that connected Jammu with Srinagar, two traversed hundreds of kilometres of territory that was to be part of Pakistan. Karachi was the traditional port of Jammu and Kashmir. Rawalpindi was the main warehouse, where nearly 98 per cent of Kashmir's non-timber exports was sent from Srinagar and Jammu. Almost the entire timber export was through trading centres in western Punjab.

Kashmir's Maharaja wanted 'Independence'

The Hindu ruler of Jammu and Kashmir did not want to join either India or Pakistan. While the departing British advised him to accede to either of the two newly emerged dominions, the Muslim League put pressure on him to accede to Pakistan and the Indian National Congress and other political groups, particularly the Hindu nationalists, tried to persuade the Hindu Maharaja to accede to India. But the Maharaja wanted to remain independent.

As the Maharaja vacillated, his subjects began to revolt. In the spring of 1947 an armed uprising broke out in Poonch, located on the borders of Rawalpindi district of West Punjab and Hazara district of the North West Frontier Province. By the third week of October 1947, the Maharaja was facing serious challenges to his authority from his subjects in the western parts of the state and in the frontier districts of the northern areas. The All Jammu and Kashmir Muslim Conference, which was close to the Muslim League and was popular in the western parts of the state and in parts of the valley, led the revolt against the Maharaja in Poonch, Rajauri and Muzaffarabad. On 27 August 1947, Sardar Abdul Qayum Khan, a local landlord, who had returned from having served in the British-Indian Army, led an attack on a police-cum-military post in Dhirkot and captured it. The event led Maharaja Hari Singh to unleash the full force of his Dogra troops on the population.

As the armed rebellion started in Poonch, activists of the Rashtriya Swayamsevak Sangh (RSS) and the Akalis mounted attacks on villages of the eastern Jammu district, killing Muslims and setting their houses on fire. This was the beginning of a widespread extermination of Muslims in Jammu in 1947. From September 1947 onwards, organised gangs of extremist Hindus and Sikhs, who were mobilised by the RSS, started killing Muslims on a massive scale. The killing was aided and abetted by the Maharaja's forces. The RSS had shifted its office from Amritsar to Jammu in August that year.

A two-member team, jointly appointed by both the Indian and Pakistani governments to investigate seven major incidents of communal killings which had taken place from 20 October to 9 November 1947 reported that about 70,000 people were killed in Jammu. The estimates of the number of Muslims killed vary: Ian Copland[49] estimated the total deaths to be around 80,000, while Ved Bhasin, the editor of *Kashmir Times*, who witnessed the communal violence in Jammu, put the death toll of Muslims around 100,000. Christopher Snedden[50] on the other hand says that the number of Muslims killed was between 20,000 and 100,000. Subsequently, many non-Muslims, estimated at over 20,000, were massacred by Pakistani tribesmen and soldiers, in the Mirpur region. In Rajouri and Poonch, many Hindus and Sikhs were also massacred by Muslim rebels.

On 24 October 1947, New Delhi received the news of a tribal invasion via General Gracey of the Pakistan Army who communicated the news to General Lockhart.[51]

R. L. Batra, the Deputy Prime Minister of Jammu and Kashmir, forwarded a message from the Maharaja to the Indian Prime Minister Nehru, requesting military assistance as well as a proposal to accede to India. On the same day, a second provisional government of Azad Kashmir was established

---

49 Ian Copland, *Community and Neighbourhood in Princely North India*, c. 1900-1950, Palgrave-Macmilan, 2005

50 Christopher Snedden, *Kashmir: The Unwritten History*, Harper Collins, 2013

51 Amar Cheema, *The Crimson Chinar –The Kashmir Conflict: A Politico-Military Perspective*, Lancer Publications 2014, p. 58.

at Palandri under the leadership of Sardar Ibrahim, while the rebel forces took over Bhimber. It was clear that between 15 August and 24 October Maharaja Hari Singh had tried his best to prevent the princely state's physical and political disintegration, but he had failed.

When the Maharaja acceded to India on 26 October 1947, his armed forces had lost control of nearly 70 to 80 per cent of the territory of 'his' princely domain. By then, J&K was a divided state. Kashmiri nationalists were also divided on religious, ethnic, cultural and linguistic lines. The Maharaja had very few options. It appears that by encouraging his Hindu subjects and the Sikh and Hindu refugees to kill and drive out the Muslim population of Jammu, the Maharaja had been trying to consolidate his hold over that area while appealing to the Indian government for military assistance to secure his hold over other areas and recover whatever other territories the Indian army could secure.

The Maharaja Accedes to India in Exchange for Military Assistance

On 25 October 1947,the Defence Committee of the Government of India, after discussing the Kashmir Maharaja's request for military assistance, decided to fly V.P. Menon to Srinagar that very day to discuss various possibilities with the Maharaja. First, the Maharaja's request for armed assistance; second, the Maharaja co-operating with Sheikh Abdullah and the National Conference; and third, the Maharaja offering accession, which would be accepted after the will of the people had been ascertained. In anticipation of the answer on the first of these points, as the records show, the Chiefs of Staff were asked to examine and prepare plans for certain possible courses of action, including flying troops to Srinagar.

The instructions to V.P. Menon show that the Defence Committee had endorsed Mountbatten's suggestion that, 'when the accession was accepted this should be subject to the proviso that a plebiscite would be held in Kashmir' when the law and order situation allowed this. Mountbatten had suggested that this plebiscite should be on three choices: to join India, to join

Pakistan, or to remain independent.[52] From 27 October 1947, Indian forces began to be airlifted to Kashmir. And the first India-Pakistan war began.

The war lasted till the end of 1948. At the beginning of 1948, India took the matter to the United Nations Security Council. The Security Council passed a resolution asking Pakistan to withdraw its forces as well as the Pakistani nationals from the territory of Jammu and Kashmir, and India to withdraw the majority of its forces leaving only a sufficient number to maintain law and order, following which a Plebiscite would be held. A ceasefire was agreed on 1 January 1949, supervised by UN observers. It seems that the Indian government had expected the UN Security Council to accept India's claim that it was a victim of Pakistan's aggression. Two weeks later Pakistan denied the charges and accused India of annexing Kashmir and destabilising Pakistan in its infancy.

India and the UN

The problem began when the UN Security Council did not name Pakistan the 'aggressor'. After crafting a ceasefire line, the UN instructed the UN Commission on India and Pakistan (UNCIP) to go to the subcontinent and help the governments of India and Pakistan to restore peace and order in the region and prepare for a referendum to decide the fate of Kashmir. Holding a plebiscite under the supervision of an international body was not acceptable to the Indian government. Prime Minister Nehru had already lost faith in the impartiality of the UN. In a letter to Vijayalakshmi Pandit he wrote, 'The USA and UK played a dirty role, the UK probably being the chief actor behind the scene. I have expressed myself strongly to Atlee about it, and I propose to make perfectly clear to the UK government what we think about it. Time for soft and meaningless talk has passed.'[53]

---

52 V. H. Hodson, *The Great Divide: Britain, India, Pakistan,* Hutchinson of London, 1969, pp. 451–54. Accessed through https://archive.org/details/in.ernet.dli.2015.118583 (Digital Library of India Item 2015.118583) on 11 May 2017.

53 Iqbal Singh, *Between Two Fires: Towards an Understanding of Jawaharlal Nehru,* NMML, Orient Longman, Hyderabad, 1993, p. 90.

For the next seven years, the Government of India was engaged in several actions, both at the national and international level, primarily aimed at extricating itself from the commitment to hold a plebiscite in Jammu and Kashmir. In 1956, Prime Minister Nehru publicly reneged on his solemn commitment to plebiscite. At a press conference in New Delhi, Nehru said the circumstances had changed as Pakistan had become a part of the US military bloc after it joined SEATO and the Baghdad Pact. The Indian government also expressed its apprehension that USA had plans to set up a military base in Kashmir, pulling India into the Cold War and also undermining India's Non-Aligned position. It also claimed any position in the status quo would adversely affect the position of Muslims in the rest of India.

Indian and Pakistani Positions on Kashmir

Thus, while Pakistan continued to profess its acceptance of the 'plebiscite resolution', India, having initially promised to participate in the plebiscite, finally rejected it in 1954. Both Pakistan and India have since made several changes in the political structure of the portions of the territory under their control. Pakistan calls the territory under its control Azad (Liberated) Jammu and Kashmir. Technically speaking this is not a part of Pakistan. It has its own government, separate judiciary and election commission and its final status is to be decided through an internationally supervised plebiscite whenever it is held in both parts of the former princely state. In reality, however, Azad Kashmir has no independent legal and political status. It is fully controlled by the Kashmir Division of the Pakistan government. Pakistan's army selects the 'President' and the 'Prime Minister' of the area, and all political parties of Azad Kashmir have to proclaim their allegiance to Pakistan.

India, on the other hand, absorbed Jammu and Kashmir as an integral part of its territory. The Constituent Assembly of India decided that the legal fact of Jammu and Kashmir's accession was beyond question and included Jammu and Kashmir among the part 'B' states of India. However, the four representatives of Jammu and Kashmir to the Indian Constituent Assembly made a request that only those provisions of the Indian Constitution that corresponded to the original Instrument of Accession should be applied to the

State. Accordingly, Article 370 was incorporated into the Indian Constitution in keeping with this request. Nehru had asked Sheikh Abdullah, the head of the interim administration of J&K to conduct an election for a Constituent Assembly in 1951. When the J&K constituent assembly upheld the accession of the princely state to India by the Maharaja, the Indian government claimed that its promise to refer the matter of accession to the people was fulfilled and the accession was final.

The positions of India and Pakistan vis-à-vis Kashmir may be summed up as per the following:

Indian Position on Kashmir

1. The state of Jammu and Kashmir is now and has been since its accession to India on 26 October 1947 an integral part of the Indian Union. Nothing agreed to by India in the UN Security Council of 13 August 1948 and 5 January 1949, or in any subsequent instrument, alters this status or in any way modifies Indian sovereignty over the state.
2. The only component of the Kashmir issue legally admissible in the talks between India and Pakistan on the future status of the state pertains to Pakistan vacating the territories illegally occupied by it.
   The future status of the state is otherwise an exclusively domestic matter to be resolved within the four corners of the Indian Constitution.
3. Talks between India and Pakistan with regard to the future status of the state should be held within a strictly bilateral framework and in conformity with the Shimla Agreement of July 1972.

Pakistani Position on Kashmir

1. The state of Jammu and Kashmir is now and has been since the end of British rule over undivided India, a disputed territory. The state's accession to India in October 1947 was provisional. This understanding is formally acknowledged in the UN Security Council resolutions of 13 August 1948 and 5 January 1949 to which both Pakistan and India agreed and which remains fully in force today, and cannot be unilaterally discarded by either party.

2. Talks between India and Pakistan over the future status of the state should be focused upon securing the right of self-determination for the Kashmiri people via the conduct of a free, fair and internationally supervised plebiscite, as agreed in the aforementioned UN Security Council resolutions. The plebiscite should offer the people of Jammu and Kashmir the choice of permanent accession of the entire state to either Pakistan or India.
3. Talks between India and Pakistan with regard to the future of the status of the state should be held in conformity both with the Shimla Agreement of July 1972 and the aforementioned UN Security Council resolutions. International mediation in these talks should not be ruled out.

Challenge to Territorial Integrity: 'State of Exception' and AFSPA

Since its independence, the Indian state has been singularly committed to defending its territorial integrity and has strongly put down, with brute military force, any demand for separation or independence, whether it was by the Nagas, Mizos, Manipuris, the Sikhs or Kashmiris. The Nehru government passed the Armed Forces Special Powers Act (AFSPA) in 1958 to crush the Naga peoples' struggle for independence. AFSPA was the resurrection of the Armed Forces Special Powers Ordinance, which was created by Churchill and Lord Linlithghow in 1942 to crush the Quit India Movement.

While the law was enacted as a temporary measure in 1958, to put down armed rebellion by Naga militants, it has remained in force till date. In 1972, AFSPA was extended to each of the seven new states created in the Northeast—Assam, Manipur, Meghalaya, Nagaland, Tripura, Mizoram and Arunachal Pradesh. AFSPA was applied to Punjab during the Khalistan movement years between 1985 and 1994. It has been applied to Jammu and Kashmir since September 1990.

The record of the parliamentary debate in 1958, during the enactment of this black law shows that very few lawmakers spoke in opposition to the law. The lone voice of caution against the enactment of this law was that of Mr Laishram Achaw, a member from Manipur. Mr Achaw had cautioned, 'This is a lawless law... I am afraid that this measure will only sever the right of the people and harass innocent folk and deteriorate the situation (sic).' The past five decades of the application of AFSPA has proved Mr. Achaw correct. A year after the enactment of the Act, in 1959, Ram Manohar Lohia visited the Naga Hills. Speaking in the Lok Sabha about his visit to the area on his return, he said that the Indian army was 'indulging in an orgy of murder and rape in the area.'

AFSPA gives enormous powers to the members of the armed forces. First, the Act allows 'any commissioned officer, warrant officer, non-commissioned officer or any other person of equivalent rank in the armed forces' to fire 'even to the causing of death' upon any person acting in contravention of any law or order, any person carrying weapons or anything capable of being used as a weapon, and to prohibit the assembly of more than five people' (Ministry of Home Affairs 1958/1998, Section 4a).

Second, the Act allows armed forces personnel to arrest without warrant and with any necessary force 'any person who has committed a cognizable offence or against whom a reasonable suspicion exists that he has committed or is about to commit a cognizable offence' (Ministry of Home Affairs 1958/1998, Section 4c).

Third, the Act allows armed forces personnel to enter and search any premises without a warrant to 'make any such arrest' (Ministry of Home Affairs 1958/1998, Section 4d). Once a person has been arrested under the Act, Section 5 instructs that they only be handed over to the police with 'the least possible delay', although this was amended in 1997 to recommend that persons arrested be brought before a district magistrate within 24 hours, excluding transportation time.

The most significant part of the Act is Section 6, which states; 'No prosecution, suit or other legal proceeding shall be instituted, except with the previous sanction of the Central Government, against any person in respect of anything done or purported to be done in exercise of the powers conferred by this Act (Ministry of Home Affairs 1958/1998, Section 6). As Lady Macbeth said while trying to wash the blood off her hand, 'What need we fear who knows it, when none can call our powers to account.'[54]

---

54 *Macbeth*, Act. V, S-1, L 32-35

It is pertinent to ask how such an extraordinary law has persisted in India's democratic polity for 60 years? During these 60 years there have been many legal challenges, review committees, and mass protests against this extraordinary black law which violates the most fundamental right—the right to life. Other extraordinary laws like the Prevention of Terrorism Act 2002 (POTA) and the Terrorism and Destructive Activities Act 1985 (TADA) have been repealed in the meantime. There has been high-level parliamentary debate over the National Security Act 1980 (NSA), the Preventive Detention Act 1950, and the Unlawful Activities Prevention Act 1967/2004 (UAPA), which have led to amendments in certain cases. However, regarding AFSPA, so far, almost all the governments, past and present, have only talked about making minor revisions. There is no indication that the law will be repealed anytime in the near future.

The only possible answer is that the areas where AFSPA is applied are seen as areas of exception.[55] The Northeast, Punjab and Kashmir are areas where the native population see themselves as ethnically, culturally, linguistically and religiously different from what is known as the 'mainstream'. Their demands for self-determination/self-rule and the armed struggles launched by them are seen as a challenge to the integrity of the nation. It is seen as a state of exception where the idea of the suspension of the constitution is validated. It is this sense of 'exceptional situation' which had led the Supreme Court of India to uphold the constitutional validity of AFSPA in 1997. In the eyes of the nation, people who demand separation from the nation become the other and the enemy. Thus, AFSPA is seen as essential for dealing with the 'enemy within'.

Unlike the self-determination movements of the Nagas, Mizos, Manipuris and the Sikhs, the situation in Kashmir is complicated further by the involvement of Pakistan, which lays a claim on the entire territory of Jammu and Kashmir because of its Muslim majority. The Kashmiris, particularly the majority Muslim population, are suspected of being pro-Pakistan. Right

55. See Girogio Agamben, *'A Brief History of State Of Exception'*, http://www.press.uchicago.edu/Misc/Chica Accessed on 18 June 2017.

from the beginning, Indian policymakers believed that sections of Kashmiri Muslims are complicit in Pakistan's desire to destabilise India. It is clear that from 1947/48 New Delhi has been following a policy of maintaining complete control over the affairs of the state and the people in various ways—manipulating elections, imposing New Delhi's chosen persons as heads of government, forcing non-Kashmiri administrators and police chiefs on the state, using the intelligence agencies to keep tabs on Kashmiri intellectuals, academics and political workers, and using the security forces to crush all political movements in Kashmir. It is apparent that New Delhi's policy was based on the assumption that if sufficient amount of non-coercive forms of inducements and force are used, the Kashmiris will finally fall in line and Pakistan will give up its dream.

Nearly seven decades down the line, the policy does not seem to have achieved any success. All the dialogues, negotiations between various political leaders of Kashmir and Indian governments, the promise of autonomy, development packages and other incentives have failed to bring about the desired assimilation and integration. The Kashmiris continue to demand the referendum or the plebiscite that was promised to them soon after Indian independence.

1990s—The Rise of Militancy

Let us return for a moment to the start of militant rebellion in Kashmir. In 1987, Kashmiri youths had participated in the state elections held that year with great enthusiasm and seriousness and fielded several candidates under the banner of the Muslim United Front (MUF). However, their hopes for a free and fair election were destroyed by the police, which had unleashed violence on their candidates and polling agents. Massive rigging of the polls by the National Conference, the Indian National Congress and Indian state agencies resulted in the total rout of MUF candidates. The poll results left a bitter trail of resentment and anger and fuelled the determination to fight violence with violence among the youth. One such young man was Mohammad Afzal Guru, then about 20 years old, who subsequently joined the militant Jammu and Kashmir Liberation Front (JKLF) and crossed the Line of Control to undergo arms training. On 9 February 2013, he was hanged for 'waging war on the Indian state'.

The movement initially had the contours of a popular struggle when in the early 1990s, hundreds of thousands of Kashmiris—men, women and children—came out on the streets demanding azadi. The Indian state, in response, sent in its army and other paramilitary forces, their numbers increasing dramatically in the interim. The local population was successfully intimidated and civilians retreated into their homes. The JKLF, which had led the azadi movement in 1989–92, declared a unilateral ceasefire, and the control of the movement passed into the hands of the separatists, many of whom were trained and funded by Pakistan.

The army and paramilitary forces clamped down severely on the valley through a sustained campaign of cordon-and-search operations, abductions, torture and killings. There were also incidents of rape and the burning down of religious shrines, residential buildings, bazaars and commercial units. Bunkers came up at every road junction, and road blocks and check posts were erected. Passengers in public buses were forced to disembark and submit themselves to frisking. People were killed on mere suspicion.

As Pakistan increasingly drove the militancy in Kashmir, the divide between ordinary Kashmiris and the militants became even more pronounced, caught as they were between the mass violence being unleashed by the Indian forces, on the one hand, and the runaway and brutal violence of the Pakistan-fuelled insurgents on the other. Pakistan initially entered as a supporter but later grew into the controller of many militant organisations which mushroomed at the time. As the agenda of the Pakistan government and its agencies played out, it also created divisions within the ranks of the militants along ideological and religious lines, as well as within the general population.

The militarisation of civilian spaces—both by Pakistan-supported militancy and the Indian state—crushed the earlier culture of open debate and discussion in the valley. The killing of several moderate Kashmiri intellectuals added to the further demoralisation of civil society. Many Kashmiris remained silent even when they realised that the strategies being followed by some of the militants were wrong, that the attacks on religious minorities in the state was condemnable and counterproductive, and that the armed groups of religious fundamentalists who had taken over the leadership of the movement were subverting the secular character and tolerant values of the Kashmiri society. These silences may have been born out of anger at the excesses of army human rights violations, or from the fear and brutalisation that violent movements tend to foster. The burden of this silence and the need to pragmatically compromise with the agencies of the Indian State for their daily needs, often led to Kashmiri being pitted against Kashmiri. Some among them began to see conspiracies and the 'hidden hand' behind every attempt to re-build civil society institutions and came to label all efforts to build a national consensus for peace and reconciliation as 'opportunistic'.

Nothing reflected the negative fallout of this failure to build a national consensus on peace and reconciliation more than the mass migration of the Kashmiri Pandit community in the wake of the militancy of the early 1990s. While many Kashmiri Muslims have frequently expressed anguish over their failure to provide their Pandit neighbours the necessary security and protection that they needed when they were at their most vulnerable and their failure to garner public support to rebuild Kashmir's syncretic society, the fact remains that the issue continues to divide the valley with no consensus emerging on the return of the Pandit community. Hard-line Hindu groups have been demanding that the government arrange for the return of the Kashmiri Pandits to the Valley, with the creation of separate enclaves exclusively for the Pandit community. The current BJP-led government headed by Prime Minister Narendra Modi has recently proposed a plan to create in Kashmir separate townships with special security arrangements for Kashmiri Hindus. This idea had been rejected by successive Indian governments, the majority Muslim population and almost all members of the Pandit community who never left the Valley. It is an idea that spurs the spectre of forced Israeli settlements in the Gaza Strip. It has contributed further to the polarisation of discourse and created an atmosphere of mutual suspicion between various segments of society in the state.

Between 2002 and 2008, militancy had declined in the region and New Delhi could have used this opportunity to begin a new dialogue for the terms of a just and lasting peace. In 2002, the BJP-led NDA government at the centre could have given Mufti Saeed's policy of a 'healing touch' full political, financial and tactical support. Unfortunately, it failed to do so presumably because of the pressure from the security establishment which claimed that the militants would take advantage of the policy to target their personnel.

The Beginnings of the Current Phase of Conflict

Two developments were to bring back violence into the state, this time much more widespread and stubborn. In May 2008, the Government of India and the state government of J&K decided to transfer 99 acres of forest land which falls in the Kashmir Valley to the Shri Amarnathji Shrine Board to house facilities for pilgrims who undertake the Amarnath yatra. This led to angry demonstrations and violence until the move was rescinded. In March 2010, Kashmir erupted in anger once again when Indian soldiers tried to pass off the killing of three Kashmiri civilians in Machil as having been perpetrated by Pakistani 'infiltrators'. Anger over these extrajudicial killings and lack of justice, gave birth to a spontaneous upsurge led by young people which spilled onto the streets and many youths took to pelting the police and paramilitary personnel with stones. Life in the Valley came to a virtual standstill as anti-India sentiment continued to simmer. These were leaderless actions, in which the protesters in fact were very vocal in their criticism of the 'leaders' and militancy. This is a fact that seemed to have been missed by the security forces and intelligence agencies which termed these mass protests as 'agitational terrorism'. With the Armed Forces Special Powers Act (AFSPA) providing them the licence to conduct themselves with impunity, uniformed personnel did not hesitate to deploy maximum force to crush civilian protests. Over 100 unarmed youth who were throwing stones died during this four-month interregnum.

Public sympathy for the militants, which was declining since 2000, revived after the brutal suppression of the stone pelting agitation of 2010. Since then, civilian support for Kashmir's militants seems to have intensified. Unlike the past, when the state's northern region near the infiltration routes was the epicentre of violence, now violent incidents are increasingly occurring in the southern part of the state with South Kashmir emerging as fertile ground for new recruits. There are reports that some have even deserted the police force to join militancy.

IV

Dealing with a Lawless State

If the security of the land
calls for a life without conscience...
Then the security of the land
is a threat to all of us

- *Paash*

There are people in other parts of India in resistance movements and they are also facing state repression and the brunt of the draconian laws. But perhaps what separates the experience in Kashmir is that the people in this resistance movement are treated not as dissenting people to be dealt with law, but as the enemy at war, and, in war, everything is fair, or so the state believes—killing, torturing, raping, disappearing, turning civilians into human shields, blinding children with pellet guns and a belligerent insistence on the refusal to talk.

The state is fighting a proxy war in Kashmir which it doesn't admit to. The heavy presence of armed forces not only at the borders but on the highways, public places, buildings, parks, cities, towns and villages, reveal a state seeking to control everyday life in Kashmir. The state claims that it is fighting a war with armed 'foreign nationals', the infiltrators, who are responsible for misleading the Kashmiri youth, that it is Pakistan-sponsored terrorism which the state is determined to crush and it is this war which is justified when the army flings bodies of those killed in the Valley in 'encounters' across the line of control or asks Pakistan to claim them before burying them in unmarked graves. In this war the state is defying with impunity the restraints that international law and constitutional provisions have imposed on how wars must be fought. The use of civilians as human shields, the destruction and blowing away of homes, and the punishing restrictions on civilian movement are all well known. Over the years, the state has also acquired special powers in Kashmir in the name of dealing with the armed insurgency against the Indian state, both through legislations and through a manufactured consent. It has acquired for itself what Ghosh (2016) calls, the 'freedom to disregard the laws of war and operate with legal immunity for military actions'. The Armed Forces (Special Powers) Act (1958), a black law operative in Kashmir, which has been discussed in some detail in the previous chapter, is firmly rooted in the colonial past and selectively applied in 'disturbed areas'. It sanctions, apart from the arrest of any person and the search of any premise without warrant, the killing of any person by the armed forces on mere suspicion.[56] The Jammu & Kashmir Public Safety Act (1978), which, according to Amnesty International (2011: 67), allows authorities 'to circumvent the rule of law', allows preventive detention for people against whom there may be no recognised criminal offence. It provides for detention for a period of up to two years in the case of persons acting in any manner 'prejudicial to the security of the state'. It further allows for administrative detention of up to one year for any person 'acting in any manner prejudicial to the maintenance of public order'. Thousands have been detained under this preventive detention law since it was enacted. In 2016 alone, as newspapers reported, some 600 detention orders were issued.

So, what do the ordinary people do in the face of this hostility? How do they respond to the vengeful war waged on them? A familiar image of Kashmir flashed across the television screens in India day after day is of violence: Kashmiris fighting, killing and dying in encounters with the armed forces, images of mass gatherings of men and, many women, of all ages, on

56 What it does not explicitly sanction but what it creates by way of condoning is also the 'right' of the armed forces to indulge in sexually assaulting women during search operations. Several reports of feminist fact-findings point to search operations as a major 'opportunity' for raping, molesting and humiliating women.

the streets, proclaiming azadi, blazing guns and pelting stones. We hear everywhere—on television debates, political parties' platforms, in homes and in public discourse—that Kashmiris have turned lawless, they have no respect for the law of the land, they are anti-nationals, and they are daring to claim a piece of the motherland. This is unacceptable to India, we are told; any one asking for a piece of the motherland will be cut into pieces. It is remarkable how across the political and class spectrum in India, the threat to 'national unity' unites India's opposition to the uprising in Kashmir. It is perhaps the faultline of the postcolonial nationalist project which produced 'national unity' in a way where sanctity of the territory became the defining principle of a sacred national identity, which the Kashmiris are seen to be harming. As a result, Kashmiri people are the 'enemy' speaking the language of disunity, violence and threatening to break the country at the behest of Pakistan, another 'enemy' which has already stolen a piece of the sacred land. On a daily basis, we encounter in State as well as media discourse, a wilfully flawed conflation of widespread, local civil society mass movement with cross-border militancy threatening to break the unity of the country. Such is the power of this discourse that crushing it with impunity is seen as natural and, indeed, legitimate.

One of the tragic outcomes of this is that the Indian people remain largely oblivious of the different expressions of resistance in Kashmir. Violence as selectively shown on the screens hides the reality of the Kashmiri uprising which grew in different forms. The peaceful communication built in Kashmir over the years, for instance, is never noticed, never broadcast on television screens and seldom picked up by the larger Indian civil society. There is a whole range of work by Kashmiri groups—mostly civil rights but also other concerned citizens who have been coming together forming coalitions, protesting in peaceful sit-ins, documenting violation of rights, building skills to defend with fact and figures, gathering hard evidence through research and ground-truthing, and screaming in silence about their grievances. Even in the face of brutal repression, Kashmiri citizens, activists and organisations have been coming together, finding new ways to resist through evidence and activism, organising and mobilising regardless of mounting restrictions on their civil and political rights. But these remain unacknowledged and largely invisible to Indians.

There has been little systematic attempt by the Indian civil society or polity to engage with these local efforts or to go into the evidence built from social facts, testimonies, and records generated through a wider participation by ordinary people. All these efforts through which unarmed Kashmiri people communicated with India, making injustices visible, sadly remained invisible to most of us, making us complicit in the crime and injustice heaped on Kashmir. However, this is a side of resistance which we must know better and respond to if we are interested in developing a true understanding of, building solidarities with, and protecting the fast-shrinking democratic space in this country. In what follows we bring together some of these unnoticed efforts of the Kashmiri people to communicate with India with reason. These are documents which are in the public domain and the initiatives mentioned are part of public knowledge in Kashmir.

* * *

Perhaps the first organised attempt by the common people in Kashmir to make themselves heard was the formation of the Association of Parents of Disappeared Persons (APDP) in 1994. APDP was formed to demand information and responsibility for the missing family members who were disappeared by the Indian security forces and presumably killed. The background to this is fairly well known. On 18 August 1990 during a raid in the Batmaloo area of Srinagar, 17-year-old Javed Ahmad was picked up by security forces from his home and was never heard from again. His distraught mother, Parveena Ahangar, an ordinary Kashmiri woman, searched for him everywhere for months together going from one police station to the next. Failing to find him, and several months into her search, she approached the high court filing habeas corpus actions seeking the whereabouts of her son who was picked up by the security personnel in front of her eyes from their home. While her son was not produced, in the process of her search for her missing son, Parveena Ahangar came across numerous other mothers, brothers, wives and parents who had lost their loved ones in similar circumstances during security agencies' crackdown as a counter-measure to tackle militancy. Their stories were similar and they realised that they were victims of the same impunity. In a large number of cases, not only were the circumstances in which their loved ones were whisked away similar, but there were also visible patterns in how the army and the police had got away with these unlawful disappearances. Some of these people came together to form the Association of Parents of Disappeared Persons (APDP) in 1994. They were supported by lawyers and human rights activists in Kashmir. Parveena became the first chairperson of the APDP and the organisation has since been fighting a peaceful battle for a little more than two decades, seeking answers about their disappeared relatives.

Every month, families of the disappeared come together under the aegis of APDP to hold a public protest in Srinagar to commemorate the disappearance of their loved ones. Holding photos of their loved ones, they get together at a public place as they seek answers from the state about the whereabouts of the missing persons. They blaze no guns and throw no stones, they sit quietly, holding photos and placards seeking information. During all these years, they have been building detailed records of those who have gone missing; more than 8,000 according to estimates since the insurgency movement began in 1989.[57] APDP has worked tirelessly to document these cases and has collected information on over a thousand cases.

Over the years APDP has expanded and there are new coalitions and partnerships developed to carry forward the task of building public memory. The Jammu Kashmir Coalition of Civil Society (JKCCS) is the result of one such partnership, as also the partnership with other organisations, one of them being the International Peoples' Tribunal on Human Rights and Justice in Indian-administered Kashmir (IPTK). Together these coalitions have been diligently working on the ground, sharpening skills and developing capacities in law, human rights, research and documentation and serious activism to build a public record through their efforts of the human costs in turbulent times.

57 On 25 March 2003, Muzaffar Hussain Baig, the then law minister informed the state assembly that since December 1992, about 3,744 persons were reported missing.

In 2009, IPTK/APDP produced a report, Buried Evidence: Unknown, Unmarked, and Mass Graves,[58] documenting 2,700 unknown, unmarked, mass graves, across 55 villages in Bandipora, Baramulla, and Kupwara districts of Kashmir. The graves investigated contained 2,943 entombed bodies of those who had conceivably died in encounters and encounter killings between 1990 and 2009. APDP's ground research was conducted between 2006 and 2009 for which it was joined by the IPTK. This report is a significant start to a systematic record of the unmarked graves where ordinary Kashmiris fear their disappeared are buried. The report found that of the entombed bodies, 2,373 (88 per cent) were unnamed, 154 contained two bodies each and 23 contained more than two, the number of bodies in each such grave ranging from 3 to 17. The Army and the Jammu and Kashmir Police claim the dead buried in unknown and unmarked graves to be unidentified foreign or Kashmiri militants killed while infiltrating the border areas on their way into Kashmir or travelling from Kashmir to Pakistan to seek arms training. However, this work which followed a complex methodology to ascertain the truth of the unmarked graves found something else.

Investigators spoke to former police officials, village heads, clerics, gravediggers and cemetery caretakers to piece together the truth. While exhumation and identification did not occur in a large number of cases, faked encounters were indeed identified. The report examined 53 cases where the bodies were exhumed from unknown graves. It was found that 49 bodies in the graves were of civilians and one was that of a local militant, while three were unknown. These people were dubbed as foreign militants by the government. Of these, following the investigations, the report found 47 to be the result of fake encounters, and evidently ordinary local citizens not connected to any militant outfits buried in these graves as foreign infiltrators.

Incidentally, this drew a dangerous parallel with the cases of disappeared Sikh youth in Punjab. During the counterinsurgency operations in Punjab especially from 1984 to 1995, there was arbitrary detention, torture, extrajudicial execution, and enforced disappearance of thousands of Sikhs. Police took away

58 http://www.kashmirprocess.org/graves

young Sikh men on suspicion that they were involved in the militancy, often in the presence of witnesses, yet later denied having them in custody. Most of the victims of such enforced disappearances never returned home and were never found again. They were killed and to hide the evidence, security forces secretly disposed of the bodies, usually by cremating them. When the state was questioned about 'disappeared' youth in Punjab, it often claimed that they had gone abroad. Later through the efforts of local investigations by human rights activists who used government cremation grounds records, over 6,000 secret cremations by the police were uncovered in just one of the (then) 13 districts in Punjab. Based on the information gathered by them, the Committee for Information and Initiative on Punjab (CIIP) moved the Supreme Court in April 1995 to demand a comprehensive inquiry into extrajudicial executions ending in secret cremations.[59]

The work done by APDP in Kashmir with the help of local volunteers uncovered the truth in a way which is almost unprecedented in recent history. There are few examples of this scale of mass graves anywhere else in India. This was no ordinary forensic evidence. This investigation linked the forensic evidence with the actions of the state to articulate a notion of public truth. The presentation of the evidence alerted the global human rights community to a new form of forensic evidence for rights violations and the *working* of impunity in Kashmir. The Human Rights Council took notice of the mass graves and reminded India of its obligations under human rights treaties and laws. Sadly though, there was not much discussion in Indian civil society on the kind of evidence that had been unearthed or on what needed to be done to stop the extrajudicial killings and get justice for the aggrieved in Kashmir. It was only a few years later, that the attention turned to unmarked graves. This happened in the 2010 case related to the killing of three young men from Nadihal village of Baramulla who went missing after they were taken to Kalaroos village in the Machil sector near the Line of Control on the promise of jobs as porters. They were killed by soldiers of 4 Rajputana Rifles near

59 For details, see, *Protecting the Killers: A Policy of Impunity in Punjab, India,* Human Rights Watch, 2007.

the Sona Pindi post and called 'Pakistani militants'. They were buried in one of those unmarked graves but their identities were revealed a month later when the bodies were exhumed on the insistence of the men's families. The state government then constituted a high-level inquiry commission to probe the killings but its report was never made public. The Machil fake encounter confirmed the evidence presented in the IPTK/APDP *Buried Evidence* report and what the Kashmiri people had claimed always—that the dead buried in the unmarked graves were local people.

In December 2012, the APDP and IPTK brought out another report, *Alleged Perpetrators—Stories of impunity in Jammu and Kashmir.*[60] This work also investigated extrajudicial executions, custodial violence, fake encounters, rape, torture, illegal detention and disappearances. Based on two years of extensive research using information collected mostly from official state documents and covering incidents from the Gow Kadal killings in Srinagar of around 50 persons in 1990 to the Pathribal encounter case in 2000, it asks why accountability for institutional crime, when the identities of the individual perpetrators are known, should not be addressed. The report is based on police records, judicial and quasi-judicial accounts and other government documents obtained through Right to Information queries, and it uses the official responses so obtained to build a record of the state of impunity prevalent in Jammu and Kashmir.

In the course of this research, the local researchers studied 214 cases and based on follow-up investigations, the report named 500 individuals: 235 army personnel, 123 paramilitary personnel, 111 Jammu and Kashmir Police personnel and 31 'government-backed militants/associates' whose complicity in the crimes of extrajudicial killings, faked encounters, torture and rape was fairly evident. The press statement on the report mentioned the evidence presented and pointed to the need for follow-up and further investigations and prosecutions to conclude the cases and bring justice to the victims and the families. However, it failed to elicit any response anywhere.

---

60 https://kashmirsolidaritymumbai.files.wordpress.com/2012/12/115733608-alleged-perpetrators-report-iptk-apdp.pdf Accessed on 20 June 2017.

In the absence of any institutional or political will to take the evidence to its natural conclusion—a trial where the crime and guilt of a perpetrator could be proven beyond doubt—the findings of the report remained un-investigated.

This work is both painstaking and significant as there are fewer studies to attempt such a detailed empirical enquiry of violations and impunity in Kashmir. It presented the identities of individual members of state forces to build a record of abuse of power and for seeking accountability for institutional criminality. By naming names, as the report said, it removed the veil of anonymity and secrecy that has sustained impunity: 'Only when the specificity of each act of violation is uncovered can institutions be stopped from providing the violators a cover of impunity.' The report indicted the Indian state of institutional and political complicity in the crimes against Kashmiri people. While this local effort helped to identify the guilty and presented the evidence of wrongdoing, there was hardly any attempt anywhere in India to engage with the evidence. There was no commission of inquiry sought, and no proposal to ascertain the evidence presented mooted in India. The only relevant news pieces that trickled in via non-mainstream media in months and years following this report were about the safe passages to the government, police and army personnel against whom there was compelling evidence presented in the report.

Two years later, in 2015, APDP and IPTK released another report, *Structures of Violence: the Indian State in Jammu and Kashmir*.[61] The report investigated human rights violations committed by the security forces and specifically analysed 333 cases of enforced disappearances, extrajudicial killings, sexual violence and torture. It also brought under investigation the role of 972 officials associated with these crimes. The report, while illustrating the patterns in violence through individual case studies, identified the structure, the forms and tactics of violence of the state and challenged the narrative which presented human rights violations in Kashmir as being mere aberrations. Strong patterns of violation were uncovered in the report. While releasing the report, APDP and IPTK urged the international community to

61 Report available at www.jkccs.net.

respond to the evidence presented in it. The report lamented the lack of domestic redressal mechanisms and mentioned that 'the continuing denial of justice from the Indian state is a reason for appealing to the international community and justice mechanisms as domestic remedies have conclusively failed the people of Jammu and Kashmir', adding that 'ignoring this evidence is (akin to) endorsing the violence of the Indian State'. It appealed to the international community not to ignore the evidence presented in the report and urged it to 'bring to bear moral and economic pressure on India to recognise the paramountcy of the rights of the people of Jammu and Kashmir in this armed conflict, and its obligations to them under international humanitarian and human rights law'.

Sadly, there was no reaction from India, no TV channel carried a debate, and no anchors went to Kashmir to ask ordinary Kashmiris about the findings of the report. All the same, while these efforts were largely ignored by the Indian state and civil society groups, due to the evidence these works produced and due to the advocacy of the local groups, they contributed to building a new cadre of young Kashmiri activists, especially among students. Many young Kashmiris, including a large number of young women, used these reports and evidence presented to articulate forcefully a strong viewpoint in various fora. It is common to come across Kashmiri students on campuses across India talking about the findings from these reports, citing statistics and facts, and arguing with passion, palpably from a position of strength to which these reports and activism contributed significantly.

In 2017, the Jammu Kashmir Coalition of Civil Society (JKCCS) brought out Amarnath Yatra: A Militarised Pilgrimage. This is a research study on the Amarnath Yatra, for which the fieldwork was conducted between 2014 and 2016 in partnership with EQUATIONS, a Bangalore-based research and advocacy organisation working on issues of tourism and ecology. The study is based on data collected from RTIs filed on multiple departments, interviews with government officials in Kashmir, concerned authorities and organisations, people in Kashmir, Jammu, Delhi and Ludhiana, and secondary sources. It is a critical enquiry into religious tourism and raises questions about the role of a constitutionally secular state in the promotion and sustenance of such tourism. It argues that the Yatra underlines the undemocratic functioning of the Indian state in Kashmir and draws attention to the related issues of militarisation, land grab and resource monopolisation, communal conflicts, and ecological devastation.

Every year when the Yatra begins, both print and electronic media carry stories presenting it as an enterprise fraught with danger for the pilgrims, focusing on the harsh weather conditions and the steep climb. However, less known in India are the hardships and punishing restrictions on their mobility that the local Kashmiri people, especially residents of Pahalgam and the villages around Baltal, have been facing year after year during the Yatra months of June to late August. While we hear about the difficulties which the devotees face, we seldom hear how local people are subjected to suspicion and scrutiny by the state during these months. Excavating the history of the Yatra, this study highlights how over the years the Yatra which was a simple pilgrimage to begin with has turned into India's assertion over Kashmir, pulverising the customary rights of the local communities, such as the Bakkarwal Gujjars, to accommodate the privilege of the pilgrims. This study too remains largely unnoticed in India.

In December 2012, when the rape and killing of a young student in Delhi galvanised a widespread protest movement which reached several corners of the world, in Kashmir, a group of young women, all in their twenties, were inspired to re-open the Kunan Poshpora case, to revisit the history and to look at what had happened to the survivors of the 1991 mass rape. As is well known (to some people), on the night of 23–24 February 1991, the fourth regiment of Rajputana Rifles carried out a crackdown in the twin villages of Kunan Poshpora in Kupwara district in the Kashmir Valley. The men were taken to the village for interrogation and the women who were told to remain inside were sexually assaulted in their homes during this cordon and search operation. As per the 2012 Jammu and Kashmir State Human Rights Commission report, the men in the villages were first ordered to come out of their houses and taken to a separate location. Then members of the security forces who had 'turned into beasts' forcefully entered these houses and 'gagged the mouths of the victims and committed forced gang rape against their will and consent'. Even minor girls as young as eight years of age were not spared. For nearly 25 years the case of Kunan Poshpora was neither investigated nor heard about in any court of law except to say that the women claiming to have been raped were all lying. The re-investigation by the young Kashmiri women led to renewed activism around the issue, a PIL, and a book called, *Do You Remember Kunan Poshpora.*[62] In this work, the young Kashmiri women shared their personal lived experience of growing up in the shadow of death and examined the questions of justice, stigma, the responsibility of the state, and the long-term impact of the trauma of violence. Through this book these young Kashmiri women tried to start a conversation with the Indian feminists and asked: is rape in India punishable but rape in Kashmir justifiable when committed by men in uniform, the protectors of India's honour in Kashmir?

The same young women were also instrumental in re-opening the Kunan Poshpora case and demanding that it be re-investigated. Through their activism, they mobilised nearly 100 women from different walks of life; 50 among them joined these young women to file a PIL in 2013, even though the case had been closed as 'untraced' by the J&K police in 1991. What their work crucially revealed is the gruelling 25-year history, from 1991 onwards, and the countless number of times that the female and male victims of Kunan Poshpora have spoken and testified, be it to fact-finding teams, journalists or the investigations that officials undertook on behalf of the state, only to be left to suffer the pain of injustice over and over again. The PIL was not admitted but the civil activism of these young Kashmiri women turned many others like them into committed activists in the peaceful movement for seeking accountability. They continue to write and speak about the incident and the denial of justice in its aftermath at various fora. They hurl no stones, blaze no guns, just ask peacefully wherever they go, be it the Jaipur Literature Festival, or audiences in Delhi, or the research community in Chennai: why is there no justice for the people of Kashmir?

---

62 Essar Batool, Ifrah Butt, Samreen Mushtaq, Munaza Rashid and Natasha Rather, *Do You Remember Kunan Poshpora,* Zubaan Books,New Delhi, 2016.

Over the last 25 years, Kashmiri photojournalists have been bearing witness to the turbulent times in their land. Their documentation has produced a visual history of the troubled land, most recently brought together in an edited book *Witness/Kashmir 1986–2016/Nine Photographers*. Edited by documentary filmmaker Sanjay Kak and published in 2017, the book is a moving compilation bringing together the work of nine Kashmiri photojournalists that 'forces you to look at what you'd rather not—at the wretched, the tortured and the maimed'. In an interview, the editor said that he hopes this book will trigger a conversation and guide the reader/viewer to a place of greater empathy and feeling.

There are many other local civil society initiatives by students, women, traders, artistes and poets, the Bar Association, and NGOs, which are not chronicled here, but where local civil society has been trying to dialogue peacefully urging Indian people to have empathy. Sadly, their attempts have gone unnoticed and the concerns they raised seldom received a response.

A mention must be made here of a poignant mass appeal which went out in May 2017 by a local Kashmiri coalition called 'Survivors for Truth and Justice, Jammu and Kashmir'. The appeal was signed by 25 men and women, all of them survivors of violence at the hands of the armed forces. Several amongst them had seen their loved ones killed, tortured, disappeared, illegally detained and sexually assaulted. Others had lost children and were trying to cope with the physical and emotional pain and on top of it all, had to endure an absence of justice with the guilty rarely held responsible or punished. The appeal urged those people who cared to offer support by raising their voice against cases of injustice in Jammu and Kashmir so that they would not be forgotten or silenced. It urged Indian readers to approach relevant national or international bodies that might be able to bring some pressure to bear on India for justice. The appeal said that India was resisting 'interference' of external powers on the Kashmir issue on the grounds of the supreme right of a nation to decide what is good for its citizens. However, shouldn't then the violations of war norms and abuse of human rights be raised by the national and international community and, rightfully so, if they decide to invite international condemnation and sanctions and boycotts?

Kashmiris and other Indian defenders of rights of the Kashmiri people are often accused for 'internationalising the issue'. But if the rights of people are violated, rules of civilised behaviour are broken, what is the mechanism to address it? What do the people of Kashmir do?

* * *

These are only some of the initiatives which demonstrate the organised attempt by the local civil society actors to tell their stories, seek answers and reason peacefully. The disproportionate use of brute force against ordinary people—which has been witnessed in the Valley over the years where an entire citizenry is criminalised and moral vandalism is justified in the rest of India by saying that those who pick up arms or stones are not entitled to protection of life and liberty—thus stands discredited.

As is clear, since the early 1990s, in the face of violent anti-insurgency measures adopted by the state, including large-scale disappearances, torture, extra-judicial killings, and sexual violence, Kashmiri citizens, activists and organisations have been finding ways to resist through evidence and advocacy. During our interactions we learn how they organised and mobilised in the face of mounting restrictions on their civil and political rights. Regrettably, there has never been a systematic attempt by the Indian polity or civil society to support these local efforts or to go into the painstaking evidence generated by these groups from social facts, testimonies, and records which they built through socio-legal documentation in partnership with local communities. What such years of work of the Kashmiri people and the refusal of India to engage with it reflects is the lack of empathy and moral courage of the Indian civil society to question the handed down trope of territorial sanctity and national unity. It is worthwhile to remember what the famous Punjabi poet Avtar Paash once said about this trope: that if the security of the land calls for a life without conscience, then the security of the land is a threat to us.

The campaigns and initiatives described in this chapter present a body of work through which a different understanding of the Kashmir conflict is produced. This is the missing data which has been generated by ordinary women and men, many among them uneducated, who have come together to publicly expose the lawlessness of the state. The 'ground truth' constructed in these reports which is the result of the daily experience of the ordinary people in this war is not mentioned in any state account. They have been telling us, if we care to listen, what they have experienced. And if we do listen, we might then better understand the conflict, the state lawlessness and hatred which is an inextricable part of the state of affairs in Kashmir.

V

Kashmir and the Imagination of the Hindu Rashtra

It is impossible to comprehend the policy of New Delhi with regard to Kashmir without recognising that for people on both sides of the ideological divide in India, Kashmir has a supreme symbolic importance well beyond just the land and its people. What makes Kashmir supremely significant for both is that it is the only Muslim majority state in India. All other Muslim majority regions in undivided India (except Hyderabad which was subdued) joined the union of Pakistan. Kashmir, through a historical default, remained with India.

For secular Indians, Kashmir is a test-case for a country that declares in its constitution that the nation belongs equally to people of every faith. By that tenet, the fact that Kashmir has an overwhelmingly Muslim population is irrelevant to the claims that Pakistan lays on Kashmir, on the grounds that the majority of its people are Muslim; because Pakistan is a country whose central organising principle is religion while for India it is not. The problem is of course the gaping chasm between the principle and practice of India's constitutional secularism. If the majority of Muslims in Kashmir are not convinced that India in practice assures them the dignity and protection of equal citizenship, then the moral claims on their hearts and minds of India's secular constitution break down. They also shatter if the Hindu (and Sikh and Buddhist) minorities do not feel safe and equal in Kashmir. The exodus of the

Kashmiri Pandits from the valley in the 1990s, and the lack of any effective political and social initiative from the Muslim residents of Kashmir to either prevent their flight, or to ensure that they can return safely today and live in mixed settlements with their Muslim neighbours as in the past, further enfeebles the secular premise for Kashmir to remain a part of India.

But the greatest weakness for those who believe that Kashmir's continuation in India is the ultimate litmus test of the success and authenticity of its secular credentials is that if the majority of Kashmiri Muslims demonstrably do not want to continue to throw their lot with India's destiny, then no secular democratic principle is endorsed by holding them to India by decades of military suppression.

For the Hindu nationalists, on the other hand, precisely the fact that Kashmir is a Muslim majority state makes it suspect in its loyalty to the Indian nation. In the eyes of the RSS, in the orthodoxy of the Sangh, the Muslim is the 'enemy within'. The taming and domestication of Kashmir has therefore always been high on the RSS agenda for India as a Hindu Rasthra, the flying of India's flag in Lal Bagh central square in Srinagar. (The irony is that the RSS has long refused to fly the Indian tricolour in its headquarters in Nagpur; it flies instead a saffron flag). The annulment of Article 370 of India's constitution, which guarantees a special status to Kashmir, is one of the triumvirate of paramount demands of the RSS. The other two are the construction of a Ram Temple at the site of the Babri Masjid in Ayodhya, and a uniform civil code (again aimed to revoke the rights of Muslim men to have more than one wife or to divorce their spouse at will).

Therefore, in the present era of triumphalism in the Hindutva camp, with Prime Minister Modi's repeated impressive successes in the hustings, the suppression of any kind of popular or militant Kashmiri assertion is politically fundamental to the advance of the Hindu Rashtra. It is for this reason that the domestication of Kashmir is seen to be imperative not just for the integrity of the Indian nation, but for the triumph of Hindu nationalism.

Unlike in the erstwhile UPA administration, which also subscribed to a militarist approach to Kashmir but at the same time kept open other avenues of dialogue and development, the present administration is happy for the Kashmiri to see the Indian state mainly in the form of a menacing and unrelenting gun-toting Indian soldier.

The *Guardian* asks, 'How did India get here? How is it all right for a constitutionally democratic and secular, modern nation to blind scores of civilians in a region it controls? Not an authoritarian state, not a crackpot dictatorship, not a rogue nation or warlord outside of legal and ethical commitments to international statutes, but a democratic country, a member of the comity of nations. How are India's leaders, thinkers and its thundering televised custodians of public and private morality, all untroubled by the sight of a child whose *heart has been penetrated by metal pellets*? This is the kind of cruelty we expect from Assad's Syria, not the world's largest democracy.'[63] The answer can only be—India got here because of the triumph of majoritarian nationalism: its hubris, its spectacular want of compassion.

* * *

The suppression of Kashmir is now a made-for-television spectacle, designed to both whet and assuage bloodlust in the rising ranks of Hindu nationalists, who see themselves as by definition the only authentic *Indian* nationalists. The army records videos of its military operations and successes, not just against Pakistan but also Kashmir, and hands these out to television channels which obediently, uncritically and often with a shared triumphalism relay these, portraying the unruly Kashmiri not just as the disloyal 'other', but as the *enemy*. It is difficult to recall an occasion in the past in which the army chief in India has openly held out threats to a section of the country's own civilians. General Bipin Rawat does so belligerently, aware that he is openly intimidating young citizens of his country and theirs. The army is a highly disciplined force, and its serving officers would not speak to and through the media unless they were authorised to do so. Again, we do not recall junior officers of the armed forces defending strategies such as the human shield aimed against Indian civilians in the way that Major Gogoi did on prime-time national television. As Apoorvanand observes,'That it did not shock us when

63 Waheed, 'The Indian Crackdown in Kashmir'.

Gogoi addressed the nation through the media after being decorated is a disturbing sign. Before him, and the current army chief, we do not remember any army officer addressing a press conference, not even after the Pakistan Army's surrender in 1971, not after Operation Blue Star or the Kargil conflict. In all these, the army was the main actor. But it refrained from being seen as the director. It was always seen as following the civil authority. The present government is invoking nationalism to legitimise itself. It is trying to show it is the first government which backs the army. The latter is obliging by making the government's nationalist agenda its own.'[64]

Even more extraordinary is the release, presumably by Indian army sources of videos, that record their harsh coercive and violent action against protesting Kashmiris. Earlier we could have expected security forces to restrain any such public celebration of their breaking of the backs and spirits of unarmed civilians, because of service discipline, for fear of criticism by liberal opinion within and outside the country, and perhaps the sense that the violent repression of one's citizens is not something to publicly celebrate in a democracy. But no longer. Instead, these videos are circulated as evidence of army valour, and of decisive action against the unruly and disloyal Kashmiri. Mohamad Junaid says that the 'open-air theatre' of violent repression was an essential part of the strategy of the Indian security forces in the first phase of militancy in the 1990s.[65] During 'crackdowns' on Kashmiri urban neighbourhoods and villages, the Indian military would pick Kashmiri men and publicly beat and torture them. It was done in front of other Kashmiris, who were forced to gather in open spaces and watch. This served 'as a warning but also as a psychological operation to break people's will.'[66]

But he feels that the current 'visual politics' of the display of army action on social media in Kashmir is different. First, he says, it helps serve the political objective of satisfying hyper-nationalist sentiment: 'The military is

---

64 http://indianexpress.com/article/opinion/columns/indian-army-against-kashmir-stone-pelting-new-army-for-new-india-4683374/

65 'Indian Masculinity, Nationalism, and Torture Videos from Kashmir', Raiot, http://raiot.in/indian-masculinity-nationalism-and-torture-videos-from-kashmir/

66 Ibid.

matching in practice what the true desh-bakhts are asking for in their blood-curdling discourse. The videos are meant to bring the Indian nation out of the closet, and unashamedly embrace the hard reality of Indian rule in Kashmir.'[67]

The distribution of these videos, he says further, is also to reassert a fragile masculinity against the deflation he feels has taken place since Burhan Wani's killing and then on election day on 9 April 2017. 'The Indian military has become inadequate to the task of keeping Kashmir subdued, or at least this is what it reads in its assessment of the desperate nationalist mood in India. It has responded with febrile displays of violence where it used to try to hide it. For long, only images of mangled bodies of dead militants were publicly displayed to assert Indian military's masculinity. Now it is bodies of unarmed Kashmiri civilians, beatings of youths and women, the humiliation of children, and blasted houses in Kashmir.'[68]

One can agree or disagree with Junaid's harsh assessment, but the question remains. Why should the army post celebratory videos of its severe punitive action against civilians who are unarmed or armed at best with stones, often very young, and sometimes women and girls? Videos that establish that the way it treats citizens of the country is in brazen violation of human rights, the law of the land, and international law?

For retired army personnel, free from even the formality of army discipline, this is of course open season. A number of them rally their hyper-nationalist rage against the rebellious stone-pelting Kashmiri youth in noisy television studios. An Indian Army veteran, Major Manoj Arya, wrote an open letter to Burhan Wani. He describes him as 'despicable'. 'You could have been an engineer, a doctor, an archaeologist or a software programmer but your fate drew you to the seductive world of social media, with its instant celebrity hood and all encompassing fame. You posted pictures on the internet with your "brothers", all you fine young Rambos holding assault rifles and radio sets. It was right out of Hollywood.... The day you started with your social media blitzkrieg, you were a dead man. You encouraged young men of

67 Ibid.

68 Ibid.

Kashmir to kill Indian soldiers, all from behind the safety of your Facebook account. Your female fan following was delirious. You were a social media rage.... I wish we had met... (before killing you). And your parent's son is dead. Dead from a 7.62 mm full metal jacket round to the head.'[69]

* * *

All across Modi's India we find that bitter and uncompromising battle lines are drawn between people wedded to majoritarian Hindu nationalism who define themselves as true nationalists, and those who oppose their policies—the left, the liberals, and the minorities—as sadly wanting in love for their nation, as anti-national. It is instructive to note that Kashmir becomes the flashpoint, or the central contention, of many of these recent contestations, especially in university campuses around the country.

Any discussion about Kashmir which does not endorse its militarist suppression is a red rag for Hindu nationalists. In 2016, three student leaders of Jawaharlal Nehru University were jailed, and several more charged, with the grave crime of sedition, after they were alleged to have organised a meeting on the anniversary of the hanging of Kashmiri militant Afzal Guru in which pro-Kashmir slogans against India were said to have been raised. In the same year, Amnesty International India held an event called 'Broken Families' at the United Theological College in Bangalore as part of its campaign against human rights violations in Jammu and Kashmir, with well-known journalist Seema Mustafa on the panel. The audience included families of disappeared persons, those who had lost loved ones to fake encounters and people whose relatives had allegedly been tortured by security personnel. Two days later, sedition charges were filed against Amnesty's Bangalore unit after members

69 Describing himself as an 'Indian citizen', Shiv Mann responded to the major: 'Running after jobs and rearing a family is the vocation of those living in societies with a semblance of normality. In a war-zone, it is the gun that people go for.... Wani knew he was a dead man walking, so does every boy who picks up the gun in Kashmir. Wani's death could precipitate a new era of rebellion in the valley, and the people won't be doing it for popularity on Facebook, but simply to die from your bullets. You'd know that as well if you made the effort to listen rather than try to weave your own narrative for their motivations.'

of the Akhil Bharatiya Vidyarthi Parishad complained that the event had featured 'anti-national songs, raised anti-national slogans, made anti-India and anti-national speeches and raised slogans saying India's Kashmir should "go to Pakistan"'. Mustafa and many others denied the charges, but tempers remained high for a long time.

Kashmiri and outstation students fought at NIT Srinagar after India lost the World Twenty20 semi-final cricket match to the West Indies on 31 March 2016. Some Kashmiri students are said to have celebrated India's defeat in the tournament. The non-Kashmiri students inside the campus objected to the celebration, and they clashed with the Kashmiri students, leaving some people injured. The next day, non-Kashmiri students waved the tricolour on campus and tried to hoist it near NIT's administrative block. They shouted slogans like 'Bharat Mata ki Jai', 'Hindustan Zindabad' and 'Pakistan Murdabad'. The Kashmiri students in turn raised slogans like 'Hum Kya Chahte, Azadi'. BJP MP Tarun Vijay lauded the 'patriotic students' for teaching separatists 'a good lesson' by waving the national flag inside the campus. The unrest forced NIT authorities to suspend classes. Classes resumed a couple of days later, but with heavy deployment of police and CRPF personnel. But on 5 April, fresh trouble broke out as police tried to restrain a protest by non-Kashmiri students, and HRD ministry officials rushed to NIT. Kejriwal tried to beat the BJP with its own nationalist stick, by tweeting that the BJP is beating those who are 'chanting Bharat Mata ki Jai' in Kashmir, while doing the same against those 'who are not' raising the slogan in the rest of the country.[70] An assistant professor in Jodhpur was suspended for inviting JNU professor Nivedita Menon for a talk, because the ABVP complained about her observations regarding Kashmir. Two members of staff in Ashoka University were asked to leave, and another resigned, because they signed a petition expressing concern about the human rights situation in Kashmir. This in a private university that was established with the stated objective of advancing liberal education.

---

70 http://indianexpress.com/article/india/india-news-india/nit-srinagar-protests-all-you-need-to-know-about-the-unrest/

Kashmiri students in universities all across India live with not just discrimination and suspicion, but also violence and victimisation. Ten Kashmiri students were expelled from a private university in Meerut in 2014 for allegedly cheering for the Pakistan cricket team. This was followed by similar action by a private university in Greater NOIDA for the same alleged 'misdemeanour'. Many Kashmiri students from around the country recount discrimination, harassment and violence, spurred by issues like cricket, beef and the unrest in Kashmir.[71] In discussions with the authors, Kashmiri students complained that even Muslim students from other parts of India try to distance themselves from Kashmiri students for fear of being targeted as sympathetic to separatism and terror.

* * *

The Hindu nationalist rage against the Kashmiri people is built on three premises. One, that the movement continues to be a terrorist movement. Second, that it is backed by Pakistan. And third, that it is fuelled by the growing radicalisation of Kashmiri Muslims. We have seen the patent falsehood of the first two assumptions; they might have been accurate for the first phase of the Kashmiri revolt in the 1990s, but no longer.

But the third assumption—that the Muslims of Kashmir are coming out in larger and larger numbers to participate in street protests because they are being radicalised—deserves closer scrutiny. An article in *Scroll* by Kashmiri journalist Hilal Mir, asks 'Why does India consistently push the false narrative of radicalisation in Kashmir?' He observes, 'No theory has more forcefully and consistently been pushed as the one that maintains that the "weakening of Sufi Islam" and the "spread of Wahhabism" has radicalised the youth to the extent that all they seem to do is to participate in anti-India protests, post so-called seditious posts on Facebook, support the Pakistani

71 http://www.news18.com/news/india/equal-citizens-of-india-kashmiri-students-recount-threats-and-attacks-1381725.html

cricket team, throw stones, pick up arms or come in between militants and soldiers during a gunfight.'[72]

Mir points out that contrary to the assumption that protests are spurred by radical Islam, 'None of the first-rung leaders of the Hurriyat Conference is a Wahhabi.... Not a single militant in the recent past has emerged out of any Ahle-Hadith madrassa in the Valley.... The man who galvanised last year's uprising in four southern districts of Kashmir was Sarjan Barkati, a Sufi preacher. He is still in jail.'[73] 'Many observers therefore believe', he suggests, 'that creating an Islamist bogey in Kashmir is the unconscious desire of the State, if not part of the counter-insurgency project. It serves the Indian state to dismiss pro-freedom demonstrations and stone throwing by schoolgirls as an outcome of radicalisation, preferably religious, instead of having to acknowledge it as an act craving political change.'[74]

The article quotes Yasin Malik, whose organisation gave up arms in 1994. Malik recalls Mandela's answer to why the African National Congress resorted to violent means, 'that the nature of the struggle is not decided by the oppressed people but by the oppressor'. He adds, 'In 2008 Kashmir made a transition to a peaceful struggle. How did the state respond? Since then we have been shouldering the coffins of our youth. The majority of the militants who have been killed in recent times had been forced to pick up arms when the state agencies went after them and turned the lives of their families a hell for the sin of having resisted peacefully during 2008 or 2010.'[75]

* * *

The sense of betrayal and the resultant wrath felt by a majority of young Kashmiris is fuelled further by the rising tide of militant Hindu nationalism which finds many echoes in the Kashmir valley. Earlier generations of Kashmiris were less touched directly by reports of communal massacres,

---

72 https://scroll.in/article/836632/why-does-india-consistently-push-the-false-narrative-of-radicalisation-in-kashmir

73 Ibid.

74 Ibid.

75 Ibid.

movements like those to demolish the Ram Temple in Ayodhya, and evidence of discrimination against Muslims in the rest of India, than the young Kashmiri today. Perhaps it is the era of instant information at the press of your mobile phone button. But everywhere we travelled in Kashmir, we observed a far greater awareness of such developments, and discussion and agitation about them in the valley. The failure of the BJP government at the centre to rein in or punish activists who unleash violence on Muslims has only added to the feeling of alienation from India among the Kashmiri youth. When news of the mob lynching of Mohammad Akhlaq in September 2015 in Dadri, Uttar Pradesh, on the mere suspicion of his family having consumed beef, or news of Zahid Ahmed, a Kashmiri truck conductor, who was killed when his truck was firebombed after rumours that it was being used to transport beef became known, they became topics of instant outrage in the Valley. Referring to a wave of anti-minority incidents in India, Malik said to Hilal Mir: 'I find it laughable that a state which is sliding into fascism and looks the other way at the murder of minorities calls us radicals.'[76]

The decision by the People's Democratic Party (PDP), a Kashmiri party, to partner with the BJP in forming the J&K state government after the 2014 elections, has also caused widespread dismay among not just PDP's core supporters but other Kashmiris in the valley as well. Many of the people we met in the valley spoke of feeling betrayed by this politically expedient alliance, particularly since Mufti himself had during the election campaign urged voters who did not want to vote for the PDP, to opt for the National Conference or Congress, rather than the BJP.

* * *

For the young Kashmiri rebels,the use of video and phone cameras and the internet are as critical to their struggle as the stones they throw. It is not just the Indian state which is fighting a war of perception in the virtual world. Ipsita Chakravarty and Rayan Naqash ask why young Kashmiris are risking life and limb to record gunfights and rights abuses to upload on the internet.

---

76 Ibid.

The impulse during the militancy of the 1990s, they say, was to bury and hide. The instinct now is to publish and share. 'At almost every encounter, every bout of stone-pelting, every face off with the security forces, from remote villages in Budgam to the towns of Srinagar and Pulwama, they are there—young men armed with mobile cameras. The Kashmir conflict is being filmed and photographed like never before.' What motivates them to do it, to step back from the heat of protest and start filming, often at considerable risk to life and limb, we ask them. 'I just wanted to show the bravery of the stone-pelters,' said college graduate Hussain. But also a 'desire to tell their own story, cutting through the noise of a "biased" mainstream media. To keep a record, to make up for all that was lost in the 1990s. To help in the "glorification of victimhood".'

And just as the militant has removed his mask, the videographer has grown bold in the face of danger. 'Death, for people here, has become a kind of heroism, a sacrifice,' said Hussain. While some take up guns, others risk their lives to film encounters, beatings and stone-pelting. Pictures of militant funerals show cell phone screens glittering in the foreground. 'In contrast', Chakravarty and Naqash note, '(the) previous generation remembers desperately burying all evidence that could link them to militancy. It left gaps in family albums.' Today, young men on the street have become 'the new chroniclers, and record keepers, of the conflict'. Even schoolboys in Attina, a village in the hills of Budgam district, keep their cell phones handy whenever there is a clash with or action by security forces.

All popular struggles for freedom have a deep moral core. In these movements there is a strong tradition of self-sacrifice for the cause of freedom. Through their executions, the failed freedom fighters, Maqbul Bhat, Afzal Guru and Burhan Wani have emerged as martyrs. We are now witnessing the unfolding of the story of their martyrdom. It is the martyrdom of Afzal and Burhan that gave birth to slogans like, 'Tum kitne Afzal maaroge, harghar se Afzal niklega!' (How many Afzals can you kill, Afzal will be born in every home) and 'We are all Burhan'.

* * *

A number of citizen groups from other parts of India visited Kashmir in the winter of 2016, in solidarity and for fact-finding. Many of them reported that many Kashmiris they spoke to believed that although the approach of the Indian government to Kashmir has for many decades been militaristic, there is a distinct toughening in the policy of the new government—a policy of deliberate repression and pacification without dialogue. This was at times referred to by people in the valley as the 'Doval Doctrine' or the 'Modi Doctrine'. The popular perception is that the policy of the new central government is of exhausting 'the people of Kashmir and thus to subdue them'.[77] The Organisation for Protection of Democratic Rights, which has periodically visited the Valley since 1992, observed that what was distinctive about the present situation, was that earlier at least some sections of people still held on to the hope that the 'Government of India would mend its ways'. Now any such optimism has been all but extinguished. The People's Union of Civil Liberties agrees.[78] It observes that there were heightened numbers of incidents of vandalism and violence during raids by the police, security forces and the army in this period; and that 'the common people have lost faith in the ordinary democratic modes of redressal as they believe that they are heavily biased against them. For instance, no FIRs are registered against offences committed by the armed forces or the police, and even if registered there is never a fair investigation, much less prosecution. Some interlocutors condemned what they saw to be the Central government's strategy of 'letting Kashmir fester and showing the big stick when matters threaten to get out of hand.'[79]

Two carefully researched articles, one for *Frontline* by A.G. Noorani and the other by Sushil Aron for the *Hindustan Times* examine the elements of the Doval doctrine, which has a bearing on both India's foreign policy and national security. Ajit Doval, a 1968 batch Indian Police Service officer of the Kerala cadre, who retired in 2005, is reputed to be one of Modi's

77 According to the feedback gleaned in the fact- finding report of the Organization for Protection of Democratic Rights (OPDR), 22 November 2016.

78 PUCL report, which came out in November 2016.

79 Cited in a document brought out in November 2016 by the Centre for Policy Analysis (CPA).

closest confidantes after Amit Shah. After his retirement from the police, he headed the Vivekananda Foundation, which is strongly embedded in the Hindutva ideology (and has become one of the main hunting grounds for senior appointments in Narendra Modi's office). Modi appointed him as his influential National Security Advisor.[80]

Noorani suggests that one of the key pillars of the Doval doctrine is 'the irrelevance of morality'. 'Doval sought to explain the dilemma one faces between "individual morality and the value system of the state". The state is necessary. "If it is necessary, protecting itself will be its supreme role. Individual morality cannot be inflicted on the larger interest of society. The nation will have to take recourse to all means to protect itself. And in this, it cannot afford to subjugate what is in its long-term interest".'[81]

The second pillar is to valorise offence rather than defence. He says that one can 'engage (one's) enemy in three modes. One is a defensive mode. That is, you see what the chokidars and chaprasis do, i.e., to prevent somebody from coming in. One is defensive-offensive. To defend ourselves, we go to the place from where the offence is coming. We are now in defensive mode. The last mode is called offensive mode. When we come in defensive-offence, *we start working on the vulnerabilities of Pakistan* (as the archetypal enemy). It can be economic, it can be internal, it can be political; it can be international isolation, defeating their policies in Afghanistan, making it difficult for them to manage internal political lands security balance. It can be anything. (I)n defensive mode you throw 100 stones on me, I stop 90. But 10 still hurt me and I can never win. Because, either I lose or there is a stalemate. You throw a stone when you want, you have peace when you want, you have talks when you want. In defensive-offence we see where the balance of equilibriums lies.'

And the third pillar of his doctrine is paramount reliance on military might. These three pillars—amorality, offence and militarism—are dangerous

80 Praveen Donthi, 'Undercover Ajit Doval in Theory and Practice', *The Caravan,* 1 September 2017.

81 Harsh Mander, 'Why Is Taming Kashmir Essential for A Hindu Rashtra', *Kashmir Observer*, 8 June 2017.

enough if they define a country's relationship with its neighbours. But the even greater problem is that these define the way he believes that internal rebellions as in Kashmir should be handled. Every dissenting voice in the valley must be crushed with the brute force of the army, even if they are children armed with stones.

Sushil Aron dissects the specifics of Doval's Kashmir policy based on a speech he gave in Hyderabad when he was not advising the government.[82] Doval, he says, characterised the Kashmir problem as the product of the 'dysfunctional mindset' of three parties: India, Pakistan and the Kashmiri separatists. India is traditionally reluctant to embrace power, Pakistan is driven by a desire to destroy India, and Kashmiris are complicit in the latter's project. According to Doval, 'India has trouble in exercising power, in setting the agenda and changing realities in its favour. Pakistan, instead, decided the timing and terms of engaging India in war or peace, India restricted itself to defensive defence, not defensive offence.' Pakistan's mistake, he suggests, is to believe that India is weak, and Pakistan, driven by religious fervour, strong. The Kashmiri separatists, he continues, assume that international opinion is in their favour and they have great faith in Pakistan even though it does not have the capacity nor the intent to liberate Kashmir. Doval argues that the situation will change if Delhi gives up its high moral ground. 'In the game of power the ultimate justice lies with the one who is strong.'

Dovil regards the 2010 protests (and presumably the 2016 one as well) not as a spontaneous uprising by civil society but part of a well-orchestrated plan by the ISI in league with Kashmiri separatists. 'Pakistan instructed people where they should congregate, where to collect stones. There would be calls from mosques as well.' He said the protests were not peaceful; apparently, the type of damage stones can do was 'totally murderous' and therefore the security forces 'were totally justified in using the force they did'.

Doval believes that if India exercises power decisively, then Pakistan and the Kashmiris will fall in line. Apart from the use of force to quell protests,

82 http://www.hindustantimes.com/analysis/narendra-modi-is-implementing-the-doval-doctrine-in-kashmir/story-uPZfR9aNCPwFCD3VkTnWZN.html

Doval also endorses a hardline political approach with a view to conceptually reconfiguring the conflict.

However, Aron identifies fatal flaws in the Doval doctrine. It is 'entirely abstracted from the nature of lived experience in the Valley shaped by unfulfilled political aspirations, an overwhelming military presence, denial of rights of assembly, and repeated excesses over the years.' 'Pakistan's machinations and religious radicalism are,' he feels, 'factors in the Valley but they thrive in the seedbed of opportunity established by India's policy.... (T) he Doval doctrine does not differentiate between separatist leaders allegedly stoking unrest and civilians on the streets—it directs the fury of the State on the latter, thus handing out a form of collective punishment. Doval's theory assumes that a period of shock therapy will rewire the way Kashmiris think about their situation and accordingly adjust their expectations. But it underestimates what collective suffering does to social resolve; a sense of injustice reinforces the search for meaning, it will not steer individuals towards depoliticized acquiescence. Theoretically neat statist strategies that delineate outcomes on paper have rarely eviscerated morally grounded longings in history. Kashmiris can be repressed, but State violence will not tame their soul. Delhi's shock therapy has already caused untold damage to Kashmir. If persisted with, it can generate severe militant blowback within the Valley.'[83]

Daniyal sums it up accurately: 'Formulated by National Security Adviser Ajit Doval, the Union government's policy is of using only force in Kashmir, force and force alone to take back the streets from Kashmir's stone pelters.'[84] No weapon or strategy of offence is out of bounds—bullets, pellet guns, human shields—even if these outrage international and national legal and moral codes. Victory can only be assured by military might. The only objective is to win, by any means. Even if blood flows, if children are felled or blinded, if mothers weep, if liberals are outraged, if people do not vote, it

83 http://www.hindustantimes.com/analysis/narendra-modi-is-implementing-the-doval-doctrine-in-kashmir/story-uPZfR9aNCPwFCD3VkTnWZN.html

84 https://scroll.in/article/836299/the-daily-fix-modi-governments-muscular-policy-is-leading-to-disaster-in-kashmir

does not matter. India has to prevail by more and more military force, even over its own people.

It is evident, however, that the Modi government's muscular policy is leading to disaster in Kashmir, as Shoaib Daniyal points out.[85] He describes the policy as 'Only brawn, no brain.' 'Kashmir's anger is so intense, the state's political presence has nearly faded out.' It is ominous that the Srinagar bye-poll in April 2017 saw a voter turnout of 7 per cent—the lowest ever in the state. 'It is worth recalling that Kashmir was relatively peaceful in 2014. The Assembly elections that year saw a voter turnout of 66%—higher than the 2017 Uttar Pradesh Assembly election turnout of 61%. However, in only two years, mass protests have disrupted life in the Valley. Paramilitary forces responded by using shotguns on crowds', adds Daniyal.

'It is easy to see the political considerations that are driving the Union government,' Daniyal continues. 'A hardline position will help the Bharatiya Janata Party politically and please its jingoist base. Yet, alienating seven million Kashmiris will be disastrous in the long term, harming not only Kashmir but perverting India's democratic DNA.'

* * *

What are we fighting for?
'All the lonely people
Where do they all belong?'
—The Beatles

When talking to people in Kashmir about their problems and concerns one has to listen, look, and watch very carefully. It is also very useful to discern changes in narratives if one has visited the valley earlier. What people say also depends on where they come from and who they are talking to. On a visit to the valley in 1990 some of us came face to face with crowds of demonstrators

85 https://scroll.in/article/836299/the-daily-fix-modi-governments-muscular-policy-is-leading-to-disaster-in-kashmir

shouting anti-Indian slogans and demanding independence.[86] 'We want freedom' was a cry that seemed to have caught the imagination of the people of the valley. We heard people repeatedly say how the security forces had killed their relatives and molested their womenfolk and reiterated that they would sacrifice their lives for the cause of liberation. When we talked to them individually, several among them pointed out that if the Germanies can think of uniting what prevented the two parts of Kashmir from doing so. They frequently made it clear that they had no intentions of joining Pakistan.

Many of those who talked to us indicated a level of political consciousness capable of being influenced by historically important international trends. Political consciousness was also evident when they complained about the erosion of the electoral process in Kashmir, about the corrupt chief ministers who they felt were foisted on them by New Delhi. A strong sense of denial of democratic rights all through the years came out quite frequently in their angry outbursts while talking to us. Despite their highly emotional mood, they were ready for serious dialogue even with visitors like us who many among them often regard as representatives of the Indian state. The common people of Kashmir were still prepared for a dialogue with the Indian government provided they were assured of the sincere intentions of its representatives. On numerous occasions, we were reminded by them of the long history of injustices meted out to the people of Kashmir by various occupying forces over the past few hundred years!

Things have changed a great deal over the past 27 years. Suspicion has grown. Local activists and people in general are weary of 'fact-finding' teams coming on short visits from the mainland. They seem to have little faith in people like us in being able to influence the policy-makers in Delhi. The first group we talked to asked us a blunt question, 'Why have you come here?' Most of our meetings started with this mistrust. The body language and the expressionless eyes of many sitting in front of us would make us feel somewhat uncomfortable. Discomfort arising not out of fear but from

---

86 A full report of this visit is available in Tapan Bose, Dinesh Mohan, Gautam Navlakha and Sumanta Banerjee. *Economic and Political Weekly,* Vol. 25, No. 13 (31 March 1990), pp. 650–62.

a feeling that we were sitting in front of people deeply hurt and infected by emotions, weary from years of suffering and tragedy.

The amazing thing is that then they would talk, and talk. Pouring out their experiences of injustice, trauma and hurt. Gone were the long repetitions of perceived historical injustices, the callousness of past governments, manipulated elections, neglected promises, and broken national and international agreements. The focus was on the present. The blindings, cracked skulls, mutilated limbs, pellet injuries, disappearances, jailing of young boys, and the all-pervasive fear of the armed forces and their brutality. Unlike before, those injured and disabled for life were much younger and included children in their early teens.

Making sense of everything we heard in January 2017 and its implications for national and international discourse is not particularly easy. How does one separate the truthful accounts from the exaggerated ones, the real hurt from political bombast? There are several psychological factors to take into consideration. Emotions have an influence on what we end up believing. Emotions can also trigger retaliation when people are subjected to violence and injustice over long periods of time, and fear or anger can make it more difficult for them to be objective. One's beliefs are conditioned over time and consolidate as time goes on. The conflict has produced emotions that we cannot analyse in some cold rational way. In that sense, the anger, the exaggerations, and violent demands, all have a story to tell. The exaggerations just reflect long pent-up anger. Beliefs take a long time to evolve and can't be changed easily. All those we met in their twenties have only experienced violence and disruptions in their lives. It is possible that we may not be able to change beliefs easily, but it is an undeniable fact that people do change their behaviour when it is beneficial for them to do so.

Kashmir and India

It has to be understood by all Indians that the anger and frustration of the youth in Kashmir cannot be wished away or controlled by force without harming all in the subcontinent. The years of unrest in Kashmir culminating in destruction and mutilation of young men, women and children in the past year has had real consequences for the rest of the country.

Events in Kashmir seem to be changing the social discourse in India among the educated and the uneducated, the old and the young. One is reminded at this point of some passages from the book *Die Massenpsychologie des Faschismus* (The Mass Appeal of Fascism). Wilhelm Reich published the book in Germany in the early 1930s and warned against the mass appeal of politics promoting intolerance and prejudice in the name of nationalism and development. But his warnings went largely unheeded. Theodore P. Wolfe translated the book into English in 1946 and *Mass Psychology of Fascism* then became available to English-reading people. Some of us read it in the 1960s and 1970s trying to understand why western democracies supported dictatorial regimes in Asia and South America and who their local supporters were. Most of the young people in India have probably not even heard of the book today.

The world has changed in many ways since Reich wrote his book, but the political methods used to influence large swathes of people by self-appointed defenders of nationalism and 'majority religion under threat' haven't. How influential these methods are can be seen in most of our newspapers and TV channels. While some writers and columnists continue to criticise violence and unfair profiling of Kashmiri stone-pelters (as they should), most editors have encouraged reporters who present news caricaturing Kashmiris and repeating unsubstantiated claims of state and non-state spokespersons. These unfair accounts filter back to Kashmir and make things even worse.

Some years ago, an eminent American sociologist William Cousins explained how easy it is to create a ghettoised violent community.[87]

A person takes a marker with indelible black ink, goes to a city square and marks a dozen people randomly with crosses on their foreheads and goes home. He does this for a few days and retires calmly to his living room. Out of the dozens of people he has marked, just by chance alone, one could turn out to be a pickpocket. As soon as he commits his next crime, witnesses will

87 Dinesh Mohan, 'Road to Perdition', *DNA*, 9 October 2008.

report that the perpetrator had a cross on the forehead. A few weeks later, again by chance, a person with a cross on the forehead (PWCF) will get into an argument and beat up a shopkeeper and sometime later one might even rape someone. Now the newspapers will report that PWCFs are becoming a social menace and must be put in their place.

This development alarms all the PWCFs who have nothing to do with each other to call a meeting for starting a solidarity society. These strangers then become a group, come to know each other well and tell each other of all the real or imaginary discrimination they face. Their frequent meetings eventually attract the attention of intelligence agencies and one of them gets arrested for possessing anti-social literature. The public then asks for a ban of the society of PWCFs. The person with the marker can now come out and claim that PWCFs are funded by a foreign agency and assume the leadership for protecting the common people against them. Ultimately one of the hotheaded PWCF kills the person with the marker and creates fertile grounds for reprisals and counter reprisals. This thought exercise informs us in a very simple way how we can create a 'criminal' group where none existed.

William Reich tells us how jingoist nationalism can persuade the middle class to accept intolerant modes of social organisation through the spread of fear and the 'creation' of an 'enemy'. On the other hand, Cousins informs us with the help of a very simple and elegant thought experiment how all of us get sucked into supporting demands for greater policing and vengeance.

We may be heading towards precisely such a situation in our country. The inept handling of the situation in Kashmir is harming all of us and making us a less compassionate society. Civil discussion of the Kashmir issue has become difficult all over the county. Thought control through fear of censure has become common. Disruptions of seminars, vandalising of newspaper offices, and controlling communication has had their desired effect. Now students and teachers in academic institutions are scared of discussing Kashmir formally and in public. Therefore, it is not surprising that there are not many groups of idealistic, peace-seeking and caring young people in India who have come forward to offer help and aid for the children hurt and blinded in Kashmir purely as a humanitarian gesture.

Long periods of violence and disturbed lives can also destroy normative values and disturb concepts of ethical behaviour. The need to manipulate information and promote majoritarian behaviour creates a chasm between the contesting parties, dragging them further away from each other and an agreement. This is obviously happening in Kashmir and the rest of India. The style of daily reporting of events in Kashmir—stone pelting, cross-border skirmishes, surgical strikes, beheadings, Pakistan interference, attacks faced by the army—has strengthened the 'us vs them' syndrome. Conformity with the official view becomes the norm and all dissent antinational. This promotes the capricious and arbitrary suppression of dissent and labelling of critics as disloyal enemies of India.

Students and other critics of the Indian policy in Kashmir have suffered dire consequences with charges of sedition slapped against them. The debate then revolves around proof of whether they raised certain 'anti-India' slogans or waved various flags. A significant number of senior politicians in the government, well-known lawyers and judges, professors, famous actors and sportspersons, who should know better, condemn the condemned and demand proof of the act so that a legal lynching can be performed with full 'public' approval. The idea that what was said is not so important as what they actually did is conveniently ignored. The fact that most of these dissenters did not actually indulge in violence, promote violence, destroy property or violate any democratic laws becomes a non-issue. Promotion of conformity and creating an atmosphere of fear makes for a non-compassionate and undemocratic populace. It also makes it easier for the government in power to demonise individuals it does not like as well as inconvenient institutions, ideas and thought processes supported by small groups. This is poison for a democracy trying to find itself and manage its affairs in a fair and inclusive manner.

It is quite clear that how the State behaves in Kashmir not only affects the lives of people there but also affects the lives of those in the rest of the country by inculcating unthinking, unmindful negative processes eating away at the core of our decent human values. This is reflected in the responses to the incident in Kashmir when Major Leetul Gogoi tied a Kashmiri man to a jeep on 9 April 2017 as a 'human shield' in the face of what he claimed was heavy stone-pelting by an angry mob, which has been discussed in some detail earlier in this book. No one in authority at any level condemned the incident. The easiest way out for those in power would have been to say that they cannot comment until the enquiry is complete. But, they did the opposite. Attorney General of India, Mukul Rohatgi is reported to have said 'I salute Major Gogoi.'[88] Going a step further, the Indian army chief, General Bipin Rawat, justifying the action said 'The Indian Army is facing a "dirty war" in Jammu and Kashmir which has to be fought through "innovative" ways.... In fact, I wish these people, instead of throwing stones at us, were firing weapons at us. Then I would have been happy. Then I could do what I (want to do).'[89] The General's words have been supported by Arun Jaitley, the Defence Minister of India: 'We will not compromise with the terrorists and the separatists. How else should a military official deal with such a situation? He used his discretion towards national benefit.'[90]

There we are, three arms of the government in power supporting a blatantly illegal, unconscionable, and violent act against citizens of India. An act which is considered a war crime throughout the civilised world. Once they do it then thousands of people across the country from all walks of life go on to praise the act of the major and he is awarded the COAS (Chief of Army Staff) commendation for sustained efforts in counter-insurgency. What armies and insurgents do in conflict zones is well-known to all of us. While criminals own up to acts of depravity for their own reasons, usually governments and their officials hide behind lies and cover-ups to maintain a façade of decency in reasonable democracies. This in the belief that democracy is best served if the people also believe in the rule of law, some norms of ethics, and that their rulers are not venal law-breakers.

It is a tragedy that even these beliefs in democratic decency are decaying and there is little concern about the direction we are taking as a society. The

---

88 *Hindustan Times,* 25 May 2017.

89 *PTI,* 29 May 2017.

90 *Financial Express*, 25 May 2017.

veil behind which governments function seems to have been discarded in favour of a muscular majoritarian future. We as a society cannot afford to build a tolerance for plummeting human values and harbour a nonchalant attitude to injustices against people apart from our own kith and kin. We are being given a binary choice between an invented nationalism and 'sedition'. A mobilisation is taking place which may lead to a political realignment of mass anger against those seen to be outside the 'nationalist' constituency. This may hasten the further polarisation of society, culture and politics into mutually incompatible subcultures. There could be many reasons for this, but the fallout of happenings in Kashmir is all but too obvious.

Kashmir and the International Imbroglio

The conflict in Kashmir started soon after British India was divided into the independent states of India and Pakistan. The process of this partition displaced between 10 and 12 million people along religious lines accompanied by large-scale violence with estimates of loss of life varying between several hundred thousand and two million. This is not the place to go into details of the India-Pakistan conflict on Kashmir, but only to remember that a birth so devastatingly painful can only take a long time to heal. It is also not necessary that the wounds heal over time as political infections can make it gangrenous. On the other hand, well thought out efforts by leaders determined to find a solution to the conflict can provide a healing process and bring peace to their people.

It is not that attempts have not been made. Besides five high-level political summits (see Box at the end of the Epilogue), there has been a continuous exchange of scholars, Track-Two diplomacy and efforts by non-governmental organisations (NGOs) to bring the two governments and the people of the two countries together. The first prominent Track-Two initiative between India and Pakistan was the Neemrana dialogue that took place under the auspices of the United States Information Services (USIS) in 1990 and was later joined by American foundations and German NGOs. Its first meeting was held at the Neemrana Fort in Rajasthan, India, in October 1991. The group comprised former diplomats, former military personnel, media persons, NGO workers and academics from India and Pakistan. Since then, there has been a significant increase in the number of Track-Two initiatives between India and Pakistan such as the Balusa Group, Pakistan India People's Forum for Peace and Democracy (PIPFPD). Of late, some new initiatives have started, such as the Chaophraya Dialogue, the WISCOMP annual workshop, the Pugwash Conferences, Ottawa Dialogue, and so on. There exist more than 12 highly institutionalised Track-Two groups, as well as over 20 other people-to-people exchange programmes operating between the two nuclear-armed powers, with both external and internal funding.[91]

It is possible that these non-government initiatives have made it possible for some sane voices to operate on both sides of the border and maintain human contacts in this surcharged atmosphere. It is worthwhile recalling the statements issued by one of these groups, the Pakistan India People's Forum for peace and Democracy (PIPFPD), when it was formed in 1994.

The Joint Statement of Lahore, September 1994 (PIPFPD)

> At a time when the governments of India and Pakistan are intensifying mutual confrontation, with government and political leaders openly talking about the inevitability of a conflict and stockpiling of nuclear weapons, the situation in the sub-continent is on the brink of war. In a climate of hysteria forces of bigotry and religious intolerance threaten the fabric of civil society on the subcontinent. In such a bellicose atmosphere, democratic rights of the people are imperilled. There is therefore an urgent need for saner voices to prevail. A group of concerned citizens from India and Pakistan, from different walks of life, have been engaged in a process to initiate a people-to-people dialogue on the critical issues of Peace and Democracy.

91 *Track-Two Dialogue in the India-Pakistan Context.* ISAS Brief, No. 408, 23 February 2016.

> *That Kashmir not merely being a territorial dispute between India and Pakistan, a peaceful democratic solution of it involving the peoples of Jammu and Kashmir is the only way out* (emphasis added)

The Delhi Declaration, November 1994 (PIPFPD)

> The people of both countries increasingly want genuine peace and friendship and would like their respective governments to honour their wishes.
>
> Peace between the two countries will help in reducing communal and ethnic tension in the sub-continent.
>
> *A democratic solution to the Kashmir dispute is essential for promoting peace in the sub-continent* (emphasis added).

It is important to note that many groups and individuals on both sides of the border have known for decades that the issue of Kashmir is neither just a territorial dispute nor a purely law and order or a military problem. They have also recognised that a democratic solution in Kashmir is essential for both countries for ensuring both domestic and international peace. However, both official and civil society initiatives keep getting stymied by vested interests every time there is a prospect of moving forward.

This impasse has very negative consequences for the people of both nations in our international relations, both political and commercial. The worst outcome is in our relationships with all our neighbours. The most obvious is the collapse of SAARC. It is quite outlandish and preposterous that the people of SAARC nations cannot travel around economically, easily and in peace and comfort in this region. The Kashmir conflict between the two largest and powerful nations has bequeathed this fait-accompli not only to our immediate neighbours but to all others who need to deal with the both of us. So, the USA could play the Pakistan card in dealing with us in very obvious ways and other countries may take their place now.

In all international gatherings, it is a matter of some amusement and at times embarrassment that the host has to be careful about dealing with Indian and Pakistani delegates, their sensitivities and seating arrangements. So much so that international organisations at times hesitate to put us in the same regional grouping. For example, the World Health Organisation operates out of six regional offices and thought it prudent to separate the two and put India in the South-East Asia Region and Pakistan in the Eastern Mediterranean Region. This tends to strengthen the notion that we may be quite different, especially in the eyes of others.

As long as this conflict remains we will not be able to have comfortable relations with many of our natural allies in Asian and African countries. In this era of heightened Islamophobia, the problem in Kashmir gives an edge to those who would want to exacerbate the communal issue within our borders for their own narrow political and commercial interests. As long as news of Islam-baiting in India continues to appear in media internationally, we will find it difficult to maintain an innocent face. The more we are criticised internationally for our handling of the communal issue, more will be the reaction of the local vigilante groups to take revenge on the so-called anti-nationals and the seditionists, very likely with a nod of approval from the powers that be.

We have to, and we must, break out of these vicious cycles of action and reaction. It is high time we realised that our actions in Kashmir will decide who we are as citizens of this society and in the wider world. As of today, we have not been able to move forward in any positive way through bilateral attempts. Is it time to think of other ways and of others' experiences? When Tony Blair, who had spent a part of his childhood in Northern Ireland, became the Prime Minister of the United Kingdom, he was determined to find a solution to the conflict, and he brought Sinn Féin in from the cold and included them in peace talks. The then president of the USA, Bill Clinton, was a close mediator in the talks. Enemies for decades, participants in violence, the Sinn Féin, the nationalist and unionist negotiators put their many and deep differences aside and signed the Friday agreement. Similarly, the Colombian government and FARC guerrillas recently declared the final day of one of the world's oldest wars with the signing of a ceasefire agreement to end more than 50 years of bloodshed. This mediation was made possible by Fidel Castro, and Cuban president, Raúl Castro, hosted the peace talks. Venezuela's head of state, Nicolás Maduro, whose country has observer status, played an important role in encouraging FARC to sit at the negotiating table. We do not give these as ideal examples to follow, but to suggest that the most intractable problems have a way out. It is possible that mediators are crucial for the initiation and continuation of talks, provided the talks include all actors and former enemies.

Official attempts at the peace process*

Tashkent Declaration, 10 January 1966

(The Soviets, represented by Premier Alexei Kosygin, moderated between Indian Prime Minister Lal Bahadur Shastri and Pakistani President Muhammad Ayub Khan).

The declaration stated that Indian and Pakistani forces would pull back to their pre-conflict positions, pre-August lines, no later than 25 February 1966, the nations would not interfere in each other's internal affairs, economic and diplomatic relations would be restored, there would be an orderly transfer of prisoners of war, and the two leaders would work towards improving bilateral relations.

Simla Agreement, 2 July 1972

(Zulfiqar Ali Bhutto, President Islamic Republic of Pakistan, Indira Gandhi, Prime Minister India)

- The Government of India and the Government of Pakistan are resolved that the two countries put an end to the conflict and confrontation that have hitherto marred their relations and work for the promotion of a friendly and harmonious relationship and the establishment of durable peace in the subcontinent so that both countries may henceforth devote their resources and energies to the pressing task of advancing the welfare of their people.

- Pending the final settlement of any of the problems between the two countries, neither side shall unilaterally alter the situation and both shall prevent the organization, assistance or encouragement of any acts detrimental to the maintenance of peace and harmonious relations.

- Both governments will take all steps within their power to prevent hostile propaganda directed against each other. Both countries will encourage the dissemination of such information as would promote the development of friendly relations between them.

- Steps shall be taken to resume communications, postal, telegraphic, sea, land, including border posts, and air links, including over flights.

- Appropriate steps shall be taken to promote travel facilities for the nationals of the other country.

The Non-nuclear Aggression Agreement, 21 December 1988

(Rajiv Gandhi, Prime Minister of the Republic of India and Benazir Bhutto, Prime Minister of the Islamic Republic of Pakistan)

The treaty barred its signatories to carry out a surprise attack (or to assist foreign power to attack) on each other's nuclear installations and facilities. The treaty provides a confidence-building security measure environment and refrained each party from "undertaking, encouraging, or participating in,directly or indirectly, any action aimed at causing destruction or damage to any nuclear installation or facility in each country.

Lahore Declaration, 21 February 1999

(Atal Behari Vajpayee, Prime Minister of the Republic of India and Muhammad Nawaz Sharif, Prime Minister of the Islamic Republic of Pakistan)

Have agreed that their respective Governments:

- Shall intensify their efforts to resolve all issues, including the issue of Jammu and Kashmir.

- Shall refrain from intervention and interference in each other's internal affairs.

- Reaffirm their commitment to the goals and objectives of SAARC and to concert their efforts towards the realisation of the SAARC vision for the year 2000 and beyond with a view to promoting the welfare of the peoples of South Asia and to improve their quality of life through accelerated economic growth, social progress and cultural development.

- Shall promote and protect all human rights and fundamental freedoms.

Agra Summit, 14-16 July 2001

(Atal Behari Vajpayee, Prime Minister of the Republic of India and Pervez Musharraf, President of the Islamic Republic of Pakistan)

The talks and peace process collapsed and no signatures were obtained for the Agra treaty.

**This is not an exhaustive account of the negotiations and summits between India and Pakistan. Only selected items and portions of treaties and accords have been reproduced here.*

VI

The State at War with its Children

The agony of the Kashmir valley is not new. It has congealed over more than a quarter century into a land of lament, loss, rage and suffering. Every second Kashmiri has known no other Kashmir except one in which it is hard to walk two kilometres without spotting security personnel in olive green and khaki, not defending you, but defending from you.

The stones flung by children and young men—and some young woman—signal a mounting, perhaps terminal, alienation from the Indian state in the Valley, and a loss of faith in the usefulness of democracy and dialogue in altering a harsh reality.

There are many crimes that play out every day in the shadows of Kashmir. But probably none graver than what we have done to the Kashmiri people. Two young colleagues, one a law scholar and teacher, the other a human rights lawyer, Mohsin Alam Bhat and Suroor Mander, have prepared a carefully documented report 'The Purgatory in Kashmir: Violations of Juvenile Justice Norms in the Indian Jammu and Kashmir'. We cannot end our record better than to quote at length from their report, with their permission:

> Young men had always (before 2016) led the protests, but this time, there was an unprecedented involvement of boys, and eventually, girls. Some of the protestors were as young as 12 years of age. Images of children in school uniforms confronting the security forces started to circulate and receive national attention.... The security

apparatus appeared to be in a bind and soon responded with utmost force. The use of pellet guns—extensively used to deter protestors—was intensified.... But during this process, an equally sinister process of criminalization and victimization of children has remained mostly understudied: the institutional processes in the criminal justice system in relation to the juveniles in the state.... Children were being treated like adults by the security apparatus and the criminal justice system, in complete violation of the state's 2013 legislation, the Indian Constitution and international law....

Many children reported that they were arrested or 'picked up' by the police. Police was reported to enter their homes with guns, and handcuff them during the arrest and during transportation to the police station. No designated Special Juvenile Police Units or SJPUs have been created by the state.... The lack of such police personnel has led to illegal arrests and detentions as well torture during detention.... Children also reported to have been kept in the police station without separating them from the adults. The non-segregation of juveniles from adults runs counter to the international legal standards and the consistent rulings of the Indian Supreme Court.... We found that there are no Juvenile Justice Boards or Child Welfare Committees in Jammu and Kashmir. This has meant that the functions of the Juvenile Justice Board (JJBs) and Child Welfare Committee are an additional responsibility of the Chief Judicial Magistrate (CJM) of the respective district. The purpose of creating separate institutional machinery for juveniles was to decriminalize the adjudication in relation to children by introducing social workers and other professionals in the process. The failure to comply with this maintains the custodial nature of juvenile adjudication....The environment within the district courts, particularly in relation to juveniles, was disturbing. It is a common sight to find young boys waiting outside the courtroom for their cases to be called out, looking forlorn and petrified, for their fate and futures were linked to the cases they were embroiled in. Some boys we met were dressed in their school uniforms, dismayed that they had to leave their classes to come for the court hearing. One of the children told us that he comes to the court every month and is worried that he will have to give up his examinations to attend the court hearings, causing an adverse impact to his future. Another young boy had just finished his class 12 and was running pillar to post trying to get a permanent exemption from appearance from the court. He told us that if he failed to get this exemption, he would have to give up his seat in an engineering college in Punjab.

The institutional mechanisms under the juvenile justice paradigm address these concerns by decriminalizing proceedings for children. In the absence of any implementation on the ground, the children in the state are being subjected to precisely those onerous and impervious procedures that the applicable legal norms aimed to displace.... More generally, addressing adjudication through the criminal justice system—rather than by implementing the state's juvenile justice regime—frames cases on juveniles in an adversarial fashion. Since the state has the responsibility of prosecuting the accused in a case, the criminal justice system operates in the mode that places the state against the individual. The juvenile justice paradigm operates in a diametrically opposite fashion—where the state is expected to facilitate child rehabilitation. Consequently, the handling of juvenile cases by ordinary criminal courts is bound to violate juvenile rights, irrespective of the intentions of judges in such courts.

> Consequently, in a properly functioning juvenile justice regime, children may even be encouraged to accept the charges against them, since they and their families can expect a compassionate treatment by a state that promises re-integration and rehabilitation. In adversarial criminal proceedings, where the state is visibly antagonistic to the interests of the accused juvenile, this possibility does not exist....
>
> The defence lawyers told us that in many cases they do not raise the issue of juvenility for children at the cusp of adulthood (usually 16–18 years) as the procedure followed by the courts to determine juvenility is very cumbersome.... The second issue that was reported to arise often related to the inability of lawyers to raise police abuse—both procedural and substantive—in front of the judge. Defence lawyers told us that they did not inform the judge about rights violations, including torture committed by the police and security forces. They felt that revealing these concerns in the court exposed the juvenile and his family to further recrimination at the hands of the police.

The writers of this intensely shaming account of the Indian state at war with its own children, remind us of what is the politically and ethically fitting response to children who choose to fight the state.

> While many of the juveniles we spoke with stated, in absolutely clear terms, that they were never involved in protests, there is no gainsaying that some children stuck in the criminal justice system may have done so. But this fact—whether a particular juvenile was involved in protests or not—should be completely irrelevant for our assessment of the propriety of the procedures adopted by the police and security forces. The obligations created by the Indian and international juvenile justice paradigm is independent of this fact. The imperative, rather, is their interests, re-integration and re-socialization. In fact, we

> contend that the state must bear greater responsibility towards the children who have participated in the protests. Even more than the juveniles in need of care and protection, those in conflict with the state deserve compassionate attention in order to fulfil the goals of the juvenile justice paradigm. It is imperative for the state to ensure that these children in particular do not suffer from stigmatization and victimization. ...The adversarial approach towards children, whether they have participated in protests or not, further entrenches alienation and marginalization.

Instead children are treated by the Indian state, in the words of its army chief, as 'overground militants'. But their tragedy mounts further manifold when children actually do pick up arms. Days before this manuscript went to press, this news report appeared by Bashaarat Masood in the *Indian Express* appeared with the picture of a boy in a school uniform smiling into the camera. He could have been our son. The story reads:

> Ever since her 15-year-old son, Farhan Wani, left home in June last year to join the Hizbul Mujahideen, Gowhar Jan would start to pray whenever she heard about an encounter. Her worst fear came true on Tuesday, when Farhan was killed in an encounter in Pehlipora village of Anantnag district in South Kashmir.
>
> Confirming this, a police spokesman said, 'A Hizbul Mujahideen terrorist was killed in an encounter with Kokernag police and security forces in Pehlipora village of Larnoo area.... (He) was identified as Farhan Wani, a resident of Khudwani, Kulgam.' A Class XI student, Farhan had left home on the afternoon of June 14 for his Physics tuition, and did not return. A fortnight later, police told his family that Farhan had joined the Hizbul Mujahideen.
>
> Gowhar's husband, Ghulam Mohammad Wani, a school teacher, then posted a message, in English, on Farhan's Facebook wall. 'My dear son, since you left us, my

body has started to betray me. I am screaming of the pain which you have given and still believe that you will come back home.... I don't want to die but am not left with any choice. I am sorry. You will have a lot to learn but I will not be there to teach you, to scold you, to help you,' he wrote.

Wani, 52, hoped that his message would bring back his 'brilliant' son, who scored 9.6 CGPA in his Class X exams. 'About your mother, she loves you more than anybody else in this world. She didn't mind going through the pain of giving you birth because somebody told her you will be there to lift her coffin on her death. Dear son, we request you to come back and start again, and we will help you in every manner, otherwise the path which you have chosen will not lead you to anywhere other than pain, stress and betrayal, and maybe the time will come that you come back and never see us again,' he wrote.

Farhan didn't respond to his father's call, but Gowhar didn't lose hope. Speaking to the *Indian Express* last month, she said she cooked Farhan's favourite chicken dish every few days, and did not let other family members touch it. After putting it in the fridge for a couple of days, she would reluctantly serve it to the family. Then she would make chicken all over again. 'When he returns,' she said, 'there should be something he likes to eat....'

Meanwhile, police said they launched a cordon-and-search operation in Pehlipora village following intelligence inputs that militants had gathered there. While Farhan was the lone militant killed, three other militants are reported to have escaped.

* * *

We as Indian citizens need to be aware that when this new generation of Kashmiris cries out for *azadi*, it will be a constant reminder of the failure, not just of the Indian state, but Indian citizens—artists, intellectuals, scientists, students, working people, farmers in the country—to stand up and speak out in favour of the legitimate rights of the Kashmiris. They will remember how we failed them.

Kashmiri poet Agha Shahid Ali left behind this poem to speak of the sense of betrayal of the Kashmiri Pandit.

At a certain point I lost track of you.
You needed me. You needed to perfect me:
In your absence you polished me into the Enemy.
Your history gets in the way of my memory.
I am everything you lost. Your perfect enemy.
Your memory gets in the way of my memory...
There is nothing to forgive.
You won't forgive me.

Reading it today, it could be a poem we write for the Kashmiri people as a whole.

'I can't say it better than Kanhaiya (Kumar, the JNU student leader)', declared Nivedita Menon speaking to students in her university, 'who said we do not love some kind of an abstract thing and say *Kashmir hamaaraa hai lekin Kashmiri hamaare nahii hain* (Kashmir is ours, but the Kashmiris aren't). We don't want the Siachen glacier. We don't want the land of Nagaland. We want people who will want to be together and if they do not want it, it is our responsibility to make it so that people wish to stay within it. And if people wish to leave, it is the responsibility of the state and the people of this country to look inside and ask: What is wrong? We do not think that a nation pre-exists its people. It is not a piece of land. A nation is created daily. A nation is a daily plebiscite.... It is up to us to reaffirm that the nation is just, that the nation is equitable.... It is a struggle for the soul of India.'

It is imperative for every Indian outside Kashmir to be mindful of the fact that the 1.3 million pellets that were set off at unarmed citizens in Kashmir in the cruel summer and autumn of 2016 were fired in our name, yours and mine. And being mindful is not enough, we must take and accept responsibility for those 1.3 million pellets. We are told that all of this is being done to make our nation strong. It is for us that seven million people in the entire valley of Kashmir had to endure the longest curfew in their history, in all our histories, unmindful of how they lived or died, how they brought food to their children or medicine to their ailing. It is for us that children are being rounded up by men in uniform from their schools and colleges to fill their prisons. It is for us that children are being blinded in the largest campaign of mass blinding in modern times.

You may say they are not unarmed. They are fighting our soldiers with stones. Yes, they are, with stones and with the fury in their hearts. But we must ask ourselves, is it right for us to blind, maim or exterminate our children because they fight our soldiers with stones?

We are told that a nation cannot be strong if it is ethical or compassionate. These are despicable signs of weakness. A strong state is a state that is without morality or mercy.

Who will tell them how wrong they are? That it is only the weak who fell those who are weaker, whose hearts are empty of mercy, who celebrate the weeping of children. The truly strong are those who have the courage to be kind and just.

Paulo Freire writes in the *Pedagogy of the Oppressed*: 'The oppressor is in solidarity with the oppressed only when he (or she) stops regarding the oppressed as an abstract category and sees them as persons who have been unjustly dealt with, deprived of their voice, cheated...—when he (or she) stops making pious, sentimental, and individualistic gestures and risks an act of love. True solidarity is found only in the plenitude of this act of love, in its existentiality, in its praxis....'[92]

The time has come for us all to risk the plentitude of such acts of love.

---

92 Paulo Freire, *Pedagogy of the Oppressed*, Penguin.

Epilogue

Kashmir has become a battle ground where India and Pakistan are carrying out an undeclared war. The national media's focus has shifted from the Valley to the border. Photographs of grieving women and old men hugging caskets of soldiers killed on the Jammu and Kashmir border skirmish now appear on the front pages of newspapers almost every day. Dressed in battle fatigues and bullet proof jackets, Indian army jawans and personnel of the Border Security Forces are constantly moving through border hamlets and paddy fields to take position to fire across the border. Devastation is visible all around—blood stains on floors, broken windows, injured animals and splinter marks on walls. By mid-January 2018, a chain of hamlets and towns along the Indo-Pak border in RS Pura sector have emptied out. Over 40,000 villagers have abandoned their homes to escape heavy shelling by Pakistani forces. The BSF had fired over 9,000 rounds of mortar shells across the Jammu International Border over the last few days of February, as part of a 'pinpointed' retaliatory action against this 'unprovoked' firing from across the border. Bilateral relations between India and Pakistan have been virtually reduced to soldiers firing at each other across the Line of Control in Jammu and Kashmir. According to various estimates, the current strength of the security forces including army and paramilitary forces is anywhere between 6.5 lakh to 7.5 lakh. Most of the army men in the Valley are from the Rastriya Rifles, which conducts counter-insurgency operations. According to information from the region, 36 RR battalions are in Kashmir Valley and 22 more in the Jammu region. The ratio of police to people is the highest here among all the states of India.

In Nichal village in Samba district, an old man waiting to receive the body of his son felled by Pakistani bullets appealed to Prime Minister Narendra Modi to either engage Pakistan in dialogue or engage it in a full-fledged war to gain lasting peace in the region. It is the Prime Minister who has virtually frozen all high-level contacts with Pakistan and vowed to continue doing so until Islamabad stops providing all logistical support for the anti-Indian insurgency in Kashmir. There is no indication that he is going to change his stance in the near future.

Since 2014, when the BJP-led NDA government came to power, Narendra Modi has given clear indications regarding his plans for Kashmir and his position on Pakistan. Addressing soldiers in Siachen in August 2014, he said, 'Pakistan has lost the strength to fight conventional war, but continues to engage in a proxy war through terrorism.' He emphasised his government would not compromise on the Siachen Glacier, rejecting arguments made by military experts for its demilitarisation. He warned Pakistan that Indian soldiers were ready to rebuff any attempt by Pakistani soldiers on any part of Jammu and Kashmir. That drum beat was echoed in the aggressive bravado of the new army chief's euphemistic assertion that the Indian army's response to the escalating LOC fire-play would be 'adequate'.

Since September 2016, when Indian state forces launched 'Operation Calm Down' in the Kashmir Valley, the valley and surrounding areas have been under a state of siege with 24-hour curfews. The army and security forces have shut down communications and used extreme and lethal force including live ammunition and 12-gauge shotguns against funeral processions, public gatherings, and street protests. They have killed over a hundred civilians and blinded hundreds more. Operation Calm Down attempted to control the 2016 uprising not only through the overt application of armed force against crowds and protestors but also through nocturnal raids, mass arrests, and the widespread use of preventive detention law against street protesters as well as individuals whom the Union Home Minister of India referred to as the 'instigators and motivators' of protests. According to him the entire Kashmiri community, the local political leaders, civil rights activists, and trade unionists, were all instigating the youth to throw stones.

The South Asia Terrorism Portal (SATP) which compiles data from media reports, says that since the Narendra Modi-led BJP government came to power in May 2014, there has been a 42 per cent rise in militancy-related deaths in Jammu and Kashmir compared with the last three years of the second term of the Congress-led United Progressive Alliance (UPA-II). According to SATP the number of security personnel killed in militant attacks has increased from 111 in 2011–14 to 191 during the BJP's first three years in power. It also claims the number of civilian deaths in Jammu and Kashmir has also increased by 37 per cent, while militants' deaths have risen by 32 per cent.

Whenever protest movements become less intensive and daily deaths and injuries decline in the Valley, the Indian media proclaims a 'return to normalcy' in Kashmir. The cynical use of the phrase 'return to normalcy' illustrates the Indian media's approach to politics in the region. It has internalised the attitude of the state—that mass uprising is 'aberrant', that state repression in Kashmir is 'legitimate', and that a period of relative calm marks a 'return to normalcy'. The recurring escalation and de-escalation of cross-border armed hostilities and diplomatic tensions between India and Pakistan is also seen through the prism of the armed forces, that all violation of ceasefire by Pakistan is 'unprovoked' and Indian army fires back only in 'retaliation'. From the beginning of the current phase of the resistance movement in 2008, the Indian media has become clearly aligned with India's longstanding political strategy for managing Kashmir. In the autumn of 2016, when there was a pause in the street agitations in the Valley, the Indian media declared 'return of normalcy' without bothering to ask whether a place where more and more people are being killed and injured every year can ever return to normal.

Talking peace with Pakistan and working out a political solution to the Kashmir dispute is not a top priority issue for Prime Minister Modi. The

Hindutva brigade, which is his primary constituency, will not be impressed by his peace talks with Pakistan. He made his strongest anti-Pakistan comment in Jammu and Kashmir, not in Delhi, where he could have legitimately criticised Pakistan for the continued violation of ceasefire in the LoC. The 2014 state assembly election communalised Jammu and Kashmir far more than the parliamentary election. Communalisation was initiated by Modi during his parliamentary election campaign in Jammu where he brought in Pakistan for the first time in a poll campaign. The BJP had vowed to adopt a 'zero tolerance' policy on terrorism in its election manifesto released on 7 April 2014.

Prime Minister Modi, like his compatriots in the Hindutva brigade, does not believe that Pakistan has any legitimate claim on Kashmir. For him, Dr Shyama Prasad Mukherjee was 'India's first martyr of the agitation for repeal of Article 370'. Mukherjee was the founder of the Jana Sangh, which later became the BJP. In 2002, after the mass killing of Muslims in Gujarat, the RSS started a campaign to divide Jammu and Kashmir into three states along religious lines, especially a separate Jammu state carved out of Jammu and Kashmir that would belong to the Hindus. A few days later, VHP President Ashok Singhal announced that the Muslim population of the proposed Jammu state would have to leave to make Jammu an entirely Hindu state. The RSS launched the Jammu Kashmir National Front to safeguard the interest of Hindus in the state. For many Muslims of Jammu, this brought back memories of October 1947 when more than 250,000 Muslims were killed by the armed gangs of the RSS and the armies of Maharaja Hari Singh. M.S. Golwalkar, the revered ideologue of Hindutva and Akhand Bharat acted as a mentor to Maharaja Hari Singh. At Sardar Patel's request, Golwalkar visited Kashmir in October 1947 to persuade Maharaja Hari Singh to accede to 'Bharat'. Earlier in the same year, it was under the advice of Golwalkar that the Maharaja had earlier disarmed and retrenched all Muslim personnel of his state's army.

The acceptance of the Hurriyat as an unofficial representative body of the Kashmiri people by both India and Pakistan was a significant development in democratising the inter-state dialogue on Jammu and Kashmir. This was an achievement of the Pakistan-India Peoples' Forum for Peace and Democracy which since 1994 has been campaigning for the inclusion of representatives of Kashmiri people in the Indo-Pakistan dialogue on Kashmir. Allowing the leaders of Hurriyat to visit Pakistan, European state capitals and USA and presenting their position on ways to resolve the dispute was a progressive step which recognised that the voices of the peoples of Jammu and Kashmir had to be given a place in the dialogues.

The involvement of the civil society of Jammu and Kashmir, India and Pakistan in several non-official and semi-official dialogues and discussions had contributed to a change in the official positions of India and Pakistan on Kashmir. Pakistan, in its official as well as back channel dialogues had agreed to seek a solution which was different from its earlier fixed position on 'plebiscite'. The Musharraf proposal promised the most progressive out-of-the-box solution to date. With the Modi government telling Pakistan they have no business to talk to the Hurriyat leaders, the India-Pakistan dialogue on Kashmir is being pushed back to the era of volatile tension in the 1990s. Importantly, it signals to the Kashmiris the return of the old regime of intolerance, that opposition to New Delhi will be looked upon as treason.

Since late 2008, the India-Pakistan 'comprehensive peace dialogue' has been in limbo. However, till 2016, the incidents of ceasefire violations have been about 300 per year. On 28 September 2016, India responded to the Uri attack by mounting a 'surgical strike' on militant bases. After this 'surgical strike' the incidents of ceasefire violations have increased exponentially. Cross-border firings have spread to the international border in Punjab as a result of which villages on both sides of Punjab have had to be evacuated. The US endorsed India's September 2016 'surgical strike' inside Pakistan. While India asserts terrorist infiltration from Pakistan is the primary cause for ceasefire violations, Pakistan claims that outstanding bilateral disputes are the issue. Even if terrorist infiltration were to end, there is no certainty that the ceasefire violations would end. The situation is complicated by the new military belligerency which is behind the massive rise in ceasefire violations last year.

A further consequence of Washington's downgrading of relations with Pakistan in favour of India is that it has emboldened the Indian ruling elite in its dealings with Pakistan. Seizing on the deterioration in US-Pakistani relations, General Bipin Rawat, the Chief of Indian Army, issued a warning to Pakistan on 12 January 2018. He said that Indian forces were ready to call Pakistan's 'nuclear bluff' and cross the border to carry out any operation if asked by the government. Pakistan Foreign Minister Khawaja Asif responded the next day, with his own warlike message. He said, the Indian army chief's statement 'amounts to (an) invitation for (a) nuclear encounter. If that is what they desire, they are welcome to test our resolve. The general's doubt would swiftly be removed, inshallah [God willing].' Earlier in the day, Director General of Inter-Services Public Relations (ISPR) Maj. Gen. Asif Ghafoor had also responded to the Indian army chief's 'nuclear bluff' assertion by warning that India will be given a befitting response if they engage in any misadventure.

Pakistan has been stockpiling strategic nuclear weapons for several years. There are reports that it had recently deployed tactical or battlefield nuclear weapons as its first line of defence against any large-scale Indian invasion or impending invasion. Pakistan claims that India has been planning to attack them under its 'Cold Start' strategy.

Pakistan claims that US government's efforts to upset the 'balance of power' in the region have forced it to deploy tactical nuclear weapons and expand its military-strategic ties with Beijing. With the US government providing India access to its most advanced weapon systems, and Pakistan moving to strengthen its strategic ties with China, the region is increasingly being polarised which is exacerbating the danger that an impending conflict between India and Pakistan could draw in the world's great powers.

The fear that under BJP rule India will be increasingly drawn into US imperialism's game plan for extending its hegemony over this region to counter China's growing economic and military power is real. The US has always fought their wars in other people's territories bringing utter devastation to local communities and the economy. That continuous localised military clashes, can lead to large-scale war is an established historic fact. We have become so used to this perpetual cycle of instability and constant confrontation along the Indo-Pakistan border that we have lost sight of the inherent danger that it poses to peace in South Asia. As a result, despite our best efforts, the next big war in the Asia-Pacific region, like most military conflicts, may come as an apparent surprise when we least expect it. For what is clear is that the current instability in the Asia-Pacific region cannot endure indefinitely.

As we have seen in the past, when the Indian and Pakistani dialogue process on key disputes is under way, ceasefire violations come down. When governments stop talking to each other, and bilateral tensions go up, the forces deployed along the Line of Control gain autonomy and local factors tend to have a dramatic influence on ceasefire violations. Instead of resuming bilateral dialogue, which is the only way disputes can be resolved, both governments have adopted an unsustainable militarist approach which has the potential of engulfing the region in a larger war, which would cause massive bloodshed and enormous damage to both countries. The present confrontation and jingoism has to stop, it harms lives of people on both sides. War rhetoric benefits the armies of Pakistan and India, defence industries, ultra-nationalists, and religious extremists. Indian jingoism does not help Pakistan's civilian government. The Indian position is helping Pakistan's army generals and Islamists to create an atmosphere of hatred and jingoism in the country.

Admittedly it will be a Herculean task for political leaders of India and Pakistan to defuse tension and engage in peace talks again. Before resumption of peace talks, the Indian government needs to stop the use of force against protesters and begin a political dialogue with the people of Kashmir to address the grievances of the Kashmiri people. As Prime Minister Modi had once said in a speech, India and Pakistan should wage a war against poverty. For this to become a reality India needs to ensure that Pakistan's civilian government has a bigger say in Pakistani politics than the country's military generals.

It is incumbent upon the concerned citizens of both countries to lead the way by giving a joint call emphasising the absolute need for the two countries to re-establish the relations that existed at the end of the last century or the beginning of this century when both governments were talking to each other. The dialogue should however not be limited to politicians, the armies or bureaucrats. Civil society organisations of both countries must be a party to the dialogue as they alone have the capacity to persuade their respective states to alter their course.

In conclusion, we would like to recollect what Mahatma Gandhi said at the prayer meeting in Delhi on 4 January 1948:

> Mistakes were made on both sides. Of this I have no doubt. But this does not mean that we should persist in those mistakes, for then in the end we shall only destroy ourselves in a war and the whole of the sub-continent will pass into the hands of some third power. That will be the worst imaginable fate for us. I shudder to think of it. Therefore the two Dominions should come together with God as witness and find a settlement.